The *Map* of *Yearning*

NIMROD INTERNATIONAL JOURNAL

The Map of Yearning

Nimrod International Journal IS INDEXED IN
HUMANITIES INTERNATIONAL COMPLETE

ISBN: 0-9794967-5-6   ISSN: 0029-053X
Volume 53, Number 2
Spring/Summer 2010

THE UNIVERSITY OF TULSA — TULSA, OKLAHOMA

The University of Tulsa is an equal opportunity/affirmative action institution. For EEO/AA
information, contact the Office of Legal Compliance at (918) 631-2602; for disability accom-
modations, contact Dr. Jane Corso at (918) 631-2315.

Acknowledgements

This issue of *Nimrod* is funded by donations, subscriptions, and sales. *Nimrod* and The University of Tulsa acknowledge with gratitude the many individuals and organizations that support *Nimrod*'s publication, annual prize, and outreach programs: *Nimrod*'s Advisory and Editorial Boards; and *Nimrod*'s Angels, Benefactors, Donors, and Patrons.

Angel ($1,000+)
: Gary Brooks, Ivy & Joseph Dempsey, Joan Flint, Stephani Franklin, The Herbert & Rosaline Gussman Foundation, Burt Holmes & Mary Lee Townsend, Susan & Bob Mase, The Williams Companies on behalf of Elizabeth & Sam Joyner, The John Steele Zink Foundation

Benefactor ($500+)
: Marjery Bird, Marion & Bill Elson, Cynthia Gustavson, Bruce Kline, Edwynne & George Krumme, Ruth K. Nelson, Donna O'Rourke & Tom Twomey, Lisa Ransom, Dorothy & Michael Tramontana, Joy Whitman, Jane Wiseman, Randi & Fred Wightman

Donor ($100+)
: Adrian Alexander & Marilu Goodyear, Sharon Bell & Gregory Gray, Harvey & Sandra Blumenthal, Phil Bolian, Colleen Boucher, Harry Cramton, Nancy & Ray Feldman, Ken Fergeson, Joseph Gierek & Mary Young, Sherri & Stuart Goodall, Helen Jo Hardwick, Ellen Hartman, Frank Henke III, Nancy Hermann, Mary Kathleen & Douglas Inhofe, Carol Johnson, William Kellough, The Kerr Foundation, Marjorie & David Kroll, Robert LaFortune, Roberta & Daniel Marder, Geraldine McLoud, Rita Newman, Catherine Gammie Nielsen, Nancy & Thomas Payne, Kate Reeves, Patricia & Gil Rohleder, Joan & Harry Seay, Diane Seebass, Ann Daniel Stone, Fran & Bruce Tibbetts, Renata & Sven Treitel, The Kathleen Patton Westby Foundation, Ruth Weston, Marlene & John Wetzel, Penny Williams, Josephine Winter, Maria & Yevgeny Yevtushenko, Rachel Zebrowski, Ann Zoller

Patron ($50+)
: M. E. Arnold, Margaret Audrain, Mary Cantrell & Jason Brimer, Katherine Coyle, Patricia Eaton, Kimberly Doenges, F. Daniel & Kay Duffy, Laurie Fuller, Susan & William Flynn, Maria Lyda, Carol McGraw, Darlene Rough, Glenda & Larry Silvey, Krista Waldron, Martin Wing, Paul Woodul

TABLE OF CONTENTS

Editor's Note
The Map of Yearning

Nimrod's "Map of Yearning" grounds us in a place we all have been and a place to which we will certainly return. It is a cartographer's sketchbook, absent of straight lines, drawn as we walk the mountains, rivers, and roads, meeting entanglements, ferruginous, layered, yet seeded with promise. It is a map of all that we long for, and all that remains—just out of reach.

It is, therefore, not surprising that in story, poem, and essay in this issue, yearning, even to the degree of insatiable craving, is expressed in a multiplicity of designs. Often there is also reference to music and dance—preludes, nocturnes, pavanes, harp songs, and incantations. As Dmitri, in Dostoevsky's *The Brothers Karamazov*, says: "It is only from the depths we learn to sing the Ode to Joy."

Kara Oakleaf's "Loving Marie," the first story in this issue, is pure charm. It is told in the clear, innocent voice of a young boy, so out of synch with his family and one friend, he yearns for the impossible, a relationship with an image in a book, a "perfect woman" from the past—Marie Antoinette, who he discovers is not so perfect after all.

"Prelude," Peter Munro's poem, also emerges from the "tide and the weather rising" through the mind and body of a boy who feels the hunger that knows no name, as we invent and reinvent ourselves, stealing even a soul as a "souvenir" of our quest, as in Michele Ruby's story where the protagonist ultimately finds a motherly lipstick imprint from an older woman a more valuable seal of approval than the enticement of friendship from the most popular boy in the class.

Daniel Donaghy's "Touch," William Woolfitt's "Oasis Prayer," Lance Larsen's "Aeolian" speak of spiritual longing, of "being ripe for God," and the urge to make a "melody of loneliness," to make one body of many hungers, to multiply His song. This is no religion of the head only, but rather a longing for touch, for the word made flesh, for the very taste and texture of the sounds of a word that sings like an aeolian harp.

Thirsting for the home one "will always be voyaging towards," is the theme of Michael Andrews' "Stitching the Poem," and "Storms Coming," told in the voice of an ancient poet who recounts how "Odysseus sings in my veins" as he does for all voyagers.

Another voyager is found in Emil Draitser's story, "Chekhov in Brighton Beach," where Semyon, the would-be actor in exile, is driven by his craving to be on stage. Even in Russia, his aspirations were never fulfilled, but minor roles helped to satisfy his longing. He manages, at first, to excuse his failure to prosper, blaming those who categorized him as "a Jew," or "a foreigner." Like Michael Lee Phillips' "Man in the Barrel," he yearns for unachievable heights and then suddenly risks even more to stop the fall, the propulsion of desire—to shift gears, as Deborah Diemont phrases it—"trespassing the border that brings him home."

These variations on a theme in poem and story map a yearning for life and growth, for home and a spiritual sanctuary, a solid ground from which to spring aloft. Driven also by a hunger for a profession that fulfills us, a family that holds us together, these poems and stories express the conflicting desires to "burrow in" and to "catapult" outward.

Also explored is a longing: for touch; for the more complex and elusive "body of the word"; for the exact names of things that, as Denise Levertov says, lead us to a reverence for life. And, despite the yearning on so many levels, there is music, dance, and a moment when the ocean or "the fever of a sunset" brings us, as Pushkin tells us, to recognize that "My sorrow is filled with light." As Marvin Bell writes in his essay in this issue, there persists a longing to express the inner life, what "life feels like," despite the difficulty in finding the right words, the accurate words in all this "dark matter and sticky stuff."

Otto Duecker, *Do You Love Me?*, oil on board, 12 1/2" x 10"

Loving Marie

I am in love with Marie Antoinette.

❖ ❖ ❖

I found her during free period. The teacher saw me looking at
a comic book and took it away because I was meant to be studying.
I took my history book out of my bag and dropped it on the desk
from a few inches in the air so it made a loud thud. The other boys
looked at me. I ignored them and did not look back. I stuck my
finger between some pages in the middle of the book and opened it
and she was staring up from a picture in the corner.

In some paintings, the ladies' eyes follow you wherever you
go, but in this painting, Marie Antoinette looked me in the eye like
all along she'd been waiting for me to look back.

In the painting, she wears a blue dress that pinches her waist
and her skin is so pale that it blends into the lace at her collar and
her sleeves. Her cheeks, though, are pink, and when I noticed,
I felt my own cheeks turn pink, too, like we were nervous to be
meeting for the first time.

❖ ❖ ❖

My brother says you fall in love all at once, and you know
you're in love because it's like getting hit with lightning. Most
people don't fall in love from just a painting, but that's how I felt
when I found her. Like I was hit hard with a bolt of hot energy,
and all of my insides sizzled and crackled.

I did not tell my brother about Marie Antoinette, but I did
tell him I was in love. He laughed at me and said, "You're not in
love, you're just bored." He is seventeen and has a girlfriend from
the girls' school. He hides condoms inside the toes of his dress
shoes. I know he uses them because he started with twelve, and
now there are only three.

My brother has a car and he picks me up after school so I
don't have to take the bus. He says he'll give me his car when I get
my license in four years, because he has an after-school job and he
figures he'll have enough money to buy a new car by then.

When we drive home, my brother goes past the park by the girls' school and we look at the girls in their skirts. He drives slow and cranes his neck toward the window like he could kiss them from all the way across the street.

❄ ❄ ❄

Beth-Ann lives in the house behind my house.

After dinner, we like to sit on top of the picnic table in her backyard until it gets dark. Sometimes I watch Beth-Ann do cartwheels off the table. I tell her she looks like a little kid, kicking her feet over her head like that over and over again for no reason, but I don't think she cares because she keeps climbing back up and flipping off.

"Do you know who Marie Antoinette is?" I ask Beth-Ann the day after I found the painting.

She looks at me. Beth-Ann has very long brown hair that reaches down to the little curve in her back. She gets mad when someone calls her Beth instead of Beth-Ann, and she likes to look at people up close when they talk.

"She was a queen," Beth-Ann says.

"She was the queen of France," I say.

Beth-Ann nods, and rolls her eyes like she already knew.

"I'm in love with her." I can tell Beth-Ann this because she goes to the public school so she won't tell anyone, and because I know she will not laugh at me.

Beth-Ann looks at me closely. She puts her elbows on her thighs and rests her chin in her palms.

"How do you know you're in love?" she asks.

"I just know," I say. "I saw her painting in a book today, and I think she's my soulmate."

Beth-Ann nods again. "My mom dressed up like her for a Halloween party once, but I can't remember what she looked like. Is she pretty?"

"Yes," I say. "She's perfect." I tell Beth-Ann to wait, and I run inside the house to get my book.

Beth-Ann opens the book to the page I marked and studies Marie Antoinette's painting. "Yes, she's very pretty." She closes the book and hands it back to me. "Why do you think," she asks, "people never smiled in old paintings?"

"I don't know."

Beth-Ann stands up on the seat and steps up to the top of the table. "Are you reading about her at school?" she asks.

"No. I just found her."

Beth-Ann turns her head to the side and looks at me. "Do you know anything about her?"

I open the book again. "I don't have to read it to know her. I just do."

Behind me, Beth-Ann carefully walks heel-to-toe along the edge of the table. "You should at least read it if you're in love with her," she says. "She was pretty important."

"Well, she was the queen," I say. "Of course she was important."

Beth-Ann turns on her toes and faced me. "Did you know," she says slowly, "that no one really liked her?"

"That's not true," I said. "Everyone always loved the queen."

Beth-Ann shakes her head. "Do you know about the French Revolution?"

"Sure," I say, because it sounds like something I should know. Beth-Ann is smart, even though she goes to the public school.

"Well, I think no one liked the queen during the French Revolution. And she *was* the queen then, I'm pretty sure." Her voice rises and falls like she's warning me.

"Well," I say. "*I* like her. I love her."

"Okay," Beth-Ann says. She does a cartwheel from the table and lands in the grass without taking a step. Then she climbs back onto the table and sits next to me.

When her mother calls her to come inside, I stay at the picnic table with my book lying open to Marie Antoinette and look at her painting. Her lips are closed, but at the edge of her mouth there is a slight upward tilt, and the pin-point of a dimple on her chin, the kind of dimple that only appears when someone smiles, and I wonder why Beth-Ann didn't realize that she was smiling.

❊ ❊ ❊

My mother comes home while I do my homework upstairs. She wears suits and high heels at work. At home, she takes quick little steps around the kitchen as she makes dinner and her heels clack against the floor like exclamation points. My mother likes to say she brings home the bacon and cooks it too. She's good at both, I think.

❊ ❊ ❊

In my history book, it says that Marie Antoinette was tried for treason and then killed. They cut off her head. When I read that, I couldn't fall asleep. I opened my book and stared at Marie Antoinette's neck. She wears a choker in the painting, and I imagined it turning to metal and slicing through her throat until my stomach was knotted into a ball and I had to kneel down.

❊ ❊ ❊

I eat by myself at school, in the hall outside the cafeteria. When a teacher or one of the boys walks past me, I pretend to be reading and concentrating hard so they won't bother me, but, mostly, I just sit and eat and wait for the bell in a corner where it is quiet. It is lonely sometimes, but not so bad.

Now that I have Marie Antoinette, it is almost nice to eat alone in the hall. I keep my book open to her picture so we can have lunch together, and I do not even notice when someone walks past and looks at me.

❊ ❊ ❊

I tell Beth-Ann she was right; no one liked Marie Antoinette.

"I told you so," she says. Then, she looks at me and said, "I'm sorry."

I shake my head.

"Maybe it's good that you like her then," Beth-Ann says. She pushes her hair behind her shoulders and I see the white strap from her bra through her shirt.

"I love her," I correct. I look down at Beth-Ann's shoulder and wonder when she started wearing bras.

Beth-Ann nods. "Well, maybe that's good. Maybe she needs someone to love her."

❊ ❊ ❊

My mother saw the painting when I left the book on the kitchen table.

"Is this your homework?" she asks.

"No," I say. I sit down at the table and look at Marie Antoinette, my pretty girl that no one else loved, and then I blink and look back at my mother. "I was just reading ahead."

"Smart boy. So. Marie Antoinette?" she asks as she clacks over to the sink to rinse her hands.

"They cut her head off," I say.

"Yes, they did."

"No one liked her."

My mother turns off the water and wipes her hands on a towel. "Well," she says. "A lot of people think she was just misunderstood."

I close the book, hiding Marie Antoinette inside. "What do you think?"

"I don't remember that much about her, to tell you the truth. But, yes, I think she was probably just misunderstood."

"I think so too."

* * *

I read about her during free period. I found a thick book about her in the library and tried to read it all, but mostly I like seeing her paintings. Paintings when she is a little girl, paintings when she is my age, paintings with her children. She is pretty even when she gets old.

There are no paintings with men. I read about her husband the king, who did not love her, and I hoped she knew that I did.

* * *

My brother laughed when I told him I was in love because he thinks I am too young to know about girls. But I know what he does with his girlfriend from what he keeps in his shoes, and I know about looking at the girls in the park.

I even kissed Beth-Ann once. She told me after that she did not want to kiss me again, but I did kiss her once, so I know more than my brother thinks.

❊ ❊ ❊

One painting of Marie Antoinette is from right after she got married, right when she became the new queen, and when I saw it, I knew she did not love her husband because she was sad. The painter probably told her to smile, and she must have tried, but her lips are scrunched tight together at the center of her mouth and her eyes shine like water, like she's crying without letting any tears spill onto her face.

Then I saw that she wore a choker tied around her neck in this painting, too, and I closed the book.

❊ ❊ ❊

Married people, I know, don't always love each other, which is why my parents did not stay married and why my dad moved away so long ago that I can't remember him at all. I don't know why he didn't love my mom. He should have.

❊ ❊ ❊

Last year, Beth-Ann told me she loved a boy in her school named Kevin, which is why she said she did not want me to kiss her anymore. She showed me his picture, with her yearbook spread open across our laps.

Kevin has blond hair that sticks straight up, like little toothpicks growing out of his scalp. In the picture, he is looking off to the left like he's bored.

"He looks stupid," I told her.

Beth-Ann snapped the book closed, pinching my thumb between the pages. "You don't even know him."

"Sorry," I said. "Does he like you?"

"He hasn't talked to me yet," Beth-Ann replied.

❊ ❊ ❊

I fell asleep in school one day because I was up late the night before. I couldn't sleep because I was thinking about them cutting off Marie Antoinette's head. The teacher smacked the back of my head to wake me up, and I grabbed at my neck when he did it. Some of the boys laughed about it, but I don't really care about them anyway.

❅   ❅   ❅

Something a lot of people don't know about Marie Antoinette is she never said *let them eat cake*. Maybe if people knew that, they'd give her another chance.

❅   ❅   ❅

"This is the problem," Beth-Ann says one night while we sit on top of our picnic table with our feet on the seat. "She doesn't love you."

I grip the edge of the table with my fingers. "How do you know? How do you know she doesn't love me?"

"Because she's dead."

"So when people are dead, they just don't care and they don't love anyone anymore?" My voice sounds mean, and it is mean, because Beth-Ann's dad is dead. He died when she was little, but older than me when my dad left. I don't know if Beth-Ann can remember her dad.

Beth-Ann stays quiet for a minute. "Maybe they can," she says. "But they can't show you, or tell you anymore, so it's not the same. You can't have a relationship with a dead person, even if they do love you."

"I still love her."

"Maybe. But it doesn't matter if she doesn't love you back."

"Kevin doesn't love you."

"So?" Beth-Ann pulls a long splinter from the picnic table and holds it between her fingers. "I don't love him anymore," she says.

❅   ❅   ❅

At dinner, my mother asks us about school while my brother taps his fist on the table and moves his fork back and forth with his other hand. When my brother does not say anything, she asks him how his girlfriend is doing, and if they have plans for the weekend.

My brother looks at me and smiles. "Why don't you bug him about *his* girlfriend?"

My mother raises one eyebrow and turns her head from my brother to me. My face gets hot and I think about the book lying on my bed upstairs, still open to Marie Antoinette's picture.

My mother smiles at me, but her smile is nicer than my brother's, who is trying not to laugh. "Do you have a girlfriend now, or is your brother making up stories?"

"No," I snap. "He's lying."

"I thought you were in *love*," my brother says, leaning forward in his chair when he says "love," drawing out the word so it has more syllables than it needs.

"Shut up."

"Okay, that's enough," my mother says. She tells my brother to leave me alone and then says to me, "Honey, it's perfectly all right to like a girl, don't let him tease you."

I think of Marie Antoinette and how my mother found my book and said she was misunderstood, and I wonder now, as my mother looks at me, if she knows it is Marie Antoinette I love. I look at my dinner plate and don't say anything.

"C'mon, tell us," my brother whispers across the table when my mother stands up to place her dish in the sink. "It's Beth-Ann isn't it, you love Beth-Ann."

"It's not Beth-Ann!" I say, and my mother hears me and finally tells my brother to go to his room.

❁   ❁   ❁

"Do you think she knows?" I ask Beth-Ann.

"That you love her?"

"Yes."

Beth-Ann thinks for a moment. "No. How would she know?"

"She'd just know."

Beth-Ann does not say anything.

"I wish I could tell her."

❁   ❁   ❁

Marie Antoinette does not look at me from all of the paintings. In some, she doesn't seem to be looking at anything. In one, her face is turned toward me, but her eyes are looking up and to the right, away from the painter. I know she is looking at something, at someone or something just above her head that isn't in the picture.

Or maybe, I think, maybe she is just looking away from me.

❊   ❊   ❊

"Do you know what a séance is?" Beth-Ann asks one night at the picnic table.

"Yes."

Beth-Ann stares at me. "Well?" She pauses. "We should try it. We can light candles and hold hands and concentrate real hard, and if you do it right, you're supposed to be able to contact spirits."

I look at her, because I cannot tell if she is serious. She looks serious, but she looks worried too, like she thinks I might laugh at her.

"If it worked, you could talk to Marie Antoinette," she explains impatiently, "you could tell her you love her."

I stare at my feet and crunch a leaf lying on the seat. "You said it didn't matter." I wait, and Beth-Ann does not say anything. "You said she doesn't love me so it doesn't matter."

"I'm sorry," she says. She stares at her hands. "It does matter."

I nod but I do not say anything.

"I just thought you would feel better if you told her," Beth-Ann says.

❊   ❊   ❊

My father did not love my mother, and she doesn't even think about him anymore. My brother says he loves his girlfriend, but he always watches the girls in the park and tells me how he likes their skirts. Kevin did not love Beth-Ann, but I think he should have at least talked to her, because there is nothing wrong with Beth-Ann.

❊   ❊   ❊

I open my book at night and look at Marie Antoinette, because I have not seen her all day. I hope that I do not look like my brother does when he watches the girls in the park, because Marie Antoinette deserves better, and should only be looked at by someone who loves her.

❅ ❅ ❅

Beth-Ann and I wait four nights before the séance, because she says the best time for talking to spirits is during a full moon.

I can see Beth-Ann's house from my bedroom window, and I watch her and her mother moving through the house behind the closed blinds. When the lights are on, I can see their bodies like shadows through the curtains, like watching a black cat run under a streetlight in the dark. I wait until I see the silhouette of her mother turning off the bedroom light, and when enough time has passed, I see the light come on in Beth-Ann's bedroom. I watch her silhouette walk into the hall, and then Beth-Ann flickers her bedroom light on and off, on and off, and that is the signal for me to come out for the séance.

Before I go outside, I brush my teeth and comb my hair.

❅ ❅ ❅

Beth-Ann comes outside in the dark with a bundle of blankets.

"It's cold," she says. A green cap plasters her hair to the sides of her face and she wears gray gloves with the fingertips cut off.

She drops the bundle on the picnic table and it falls open. The candles hidden inside begin to roll away; we scramble to catch them and set them in two lines at the end of the table.

Beth-Ann strikes two matches and hands one to me. She quickly lights each candle on her end of the table while I burn my fingers after only lighting three wicks. Beth-Ann walks over to me and I show her my hand. She touches my fingertips where the match burned and says that I will be okay.

"Put your fingers in your mouth if they still hurt," she says. She takes the box of matches and finishes lighting my candles for me before sitting down at the table.

The flames jump up and down with the breeze. Beth-Ann's teeth chatter.

"What do we do now?" I whisper.

"Sit there," she directs. I sit opposite her.

"Now hold my hands and close your eyes." She reaches across the table, palms up. I take her hands and her gloves itch my skin. Her bare fingers, colder and smaller than mine, grip my hands.

"Now concentrate." Beth-Ann's eyes lock on mine, and she nods once before looking down and closing her eyes. The candles throw orange light across her face and the shadows from her eyelashes reach halfway down her cheeks. From her lips, I can see that her teeth are still chattering inside her mouth.

I watch Beth-Ann for another minute, but she does not move, so I close my eyes and think of Marie Antoinette. How she could look at me from inside a painting and two hundred years away. How my insides sizzled and crackled. How no one liked her and how they cut off her head. How much she wanted to know that someone loved her, that I loved her, and how that must be enough to make her love me back. It had to be.

Beth-Ann's fingers tighten around my hands.

I know her painting, the painting I'd first met her in, by heart. I pull her face up from my memory and wait until she looks at me, until I know she sees me.

A cold wind hits my face and blows the heat from the candles toward our hands. Beth-Ann jumps up and tears her hands from mine. She breathes hard, and now her eyes are wide. Beth-Ann is not usually scared.

"Did you tell her?" she asks in a raspy whisper. "Did you tell her?" Under her sweater, her chest rises and falls with every quick breath.

❊　❊　❊

I took my book about Marie Antoinette back to the library the next day, but it was already a week past the due date, and the librarian asked me for sixty-five cents. I gave her the change from my pocket and the book. She put the change in an envelope and dropped the book on a metal cart with lots of other books, and I winced at the clanging sound it made.

❊　❊　❊

I do not know if Marie Antoinette heard me at the séance or if it worked. If she was there, she did not say anything to me.

I just wanted her to sit with me for a moment.

I did not tell Beth-Ann this, but I don't think she was there.

❊　❊　❊

Beth-Ann walks out of her house in a pale blond wig, a huge mass of nearly white curls springing from her head. Her face looks smaller in the center of all that hair, like a little flower bud growing dandelion fluff.

"What is that?" I ask.

"It's a wig," she said. "Do you recognize it?"

I shake my head.

"Oh. It's my mom's, it's her Marie Antoinette wig." Beth-Ann presses her lips together. "I told you my mom wore it to a Halloween party once, remember?"

I frown. "It doesn't look like her."

Beth-Ann looks down and tugs at the hem of her t-shirt. "I guess you need the rest of the costume for it to look right."

"Why are you wearing it?" It looks uncomfortable and I can barely see Beth-Ann under the mane of blond.

Beth-Ann sucks in a breath and holds it. "I—I just wanted to show it to you. Because we've been talking about her." She climbs up on the table and sits next to me. Coarse, blond wig hairs brush my face. I scratch my cheek.

"I just thought maybe . . . maybe you'd laugh at it," Beth-Ann spits out. "Because it's kind of a funny wig, and I just thought maybe if you could laugh about it, you'd feel better."

I nod, but I don't want to laugh, not now. "Can you take it off?"

Beth-Ann pushes the wig back from her forehead and lets it drop behind her. I watch her own hair slip out from under the wig, and she looks like herself again.

Beth-Ann's hair is so long it reaches down to the little curve in her back.

❊　❊　❊

"How do you get over someone?" I ask.

Beth-Ann looks at me. "I think you just have to wait."

I nod, and think that I might have to wait for a very long time. I lie down on the table, resting my head on the wood. Beth-Ann leans back and lies next to me, propping herself up on her elbows.

After a minute, she stands up, steps over me, and does a cartwheel off the table. I turn my head and watch her land in the grass. She climbs back up and cartwheels off again. I keep watching. We stay at our picnic table for a long time.

from *Hard Weather Prayers*

Prelude

Craggy as the shell of a dog whelk,
these prayers spiral outward, ordered,
disordered, devised to help me live
with what I do not know:
When I was a boy something happened.
I am not being coy. If I knew what *it*
was, I would tell you clearly. I know
that I knew more about tide pools and the beasts
that grapple to pilings, about gulls buckling
their songs to the rain, and about the storms
that swept across the Gulf of Alaska
to crash against my little town than I knew
about the tide and the weather rising through me.
Because it happened when I was a boy, as a boy
I noted the purple slow sea-star, how it killed,
striking imperceptibly between low tide and low.
I watched the basket cockle speak ridges into its heart-
shaped armor, secreting added strength
against the claws of the dungeness crab.
I studied the names of those creatures that stayed alive
by hiding or by clamping down or by building walls
or by taking the phrases of camouflage into their skins
and striking the unwary. While I was still a child
I taught myself to hunger quietly, under cover of drama.
I taught myself the language of not knowing
and subjugated my tongue to the tongues of sea gulls,
leaving for the Holy Ghost only gibberish
out of which to carve the Word aflame,
out of which to carve the words for rain.
I taught myself to extrude my gut like the sea-star,
vulnerable and deadly and unrecognizable
and the rain veiled it all
and I worshiped the rain.

Souvenir

The text message on Will's cell was the old one: "Gerhardt: Java Jones, 11:00 Saturday. You'll receive your instructions then." Will considered texting him back with a "No can do, man," but damn, it'd be good to revisit the old days. At 10:45 on Saturday, Will bought a coffee, selected a spot near the entrance, and jackknifed himself into the plastic seat to wait.

They hadn't played the game all spring, not since Scott had abandoned Will to join the tennis team. Last semester they'd played it nearly every weekend, but now Scott practiced with the club pro on weekends—returning to his blond roots, Will had called it after Scott had ditched the brow ring and let the black dye grow out. Scott was now muscled and tan. Will was still pale and too tall for his musculature, as if he'd been built from Tinker Toys. His t-shirt flapped around him when he walked. He hung with the theatre crowd and Scott hung with the jocks. The last time Will saw Scott, he had his arm draped around the shoulder of Preston Sterling, and the two boys were laughing about something.

Will didn't begrudge Scott the new jock identity. As a military brat, Will had been in the habit of reinventing himself every year or so—new town, new crowd, new Will. When Will moved to Arlington just as his junior year was starting, Scott had been his acting partner in Mr. Seabry's theatre class. Now Scott frequently acted as if he barely knew Will. Evidently, for Scott, the history field trip to the Spy Museum was just that—history, along with the aliases they'd been given when they entered the museum—Gerhardt and Ferguson. Scott had invented the game on the ride home.

"Guess which?" Scott had begun it. He slumped against the seat, holding his backpack to his chest, closing his eyes and bobbing his head. Will looked around the Metro car. Across the aisle, an older woman was nodding off over her purse; Scott had nailed her exhaustion, down to the mouth hanging just open. Observation exercise number two from Mr. Seabry's class. "Research," Mr. Seabry had called it. "Stealing their souls," Scott called it. Then he did Will: somehow he folded his frame into the seat so his elbows and knees seemed to protrude everywhere. He hummed under his breath and cocked his head to the right—Will's pose of concentration. Will laughed, grateful for the opportunity to see what he'd look like if he were as blond and perfect as Scott.

Will did a fidgety kid a few seats up and then his scowling mother, but Scott was unimpressed. "Do your research," he said in Mr. Seabry's voice. "Follow that woman until you know her every quirk, her movement vocabulary, her very soul." Mr. Seabry was big on movement vocabulary. Will took the challenge and got off the subway when the mother did. Scott hurried after him. They followed the scowling mother to the grocery where she bought a candy bar to keep the kid quiet, a roasted chicken, a bag of salad, a half-gallon of milk, and a generic pain reliever. Back on the sidewalk, Will built into his take the woman's headache and the incessant chatter of the kid, and Scott was impressed. "Well done, Gerhardt. Now it's Ferguson's turn." And they tailed a man in a turban into the store.

The game evolved; they built backstories for Gerhardt and Ferguson, and increasingly complicated spy histories for the people they followed. They followed their marks for longer, and sometimes split up, going solo to avoid notice, making a contest out of it. Eventually, the stakes were raised, and some proof was required. That was Scott's specialty—raising the stakes.

At 11:01, Scott strolled past, bumped into Will's chair, said, "Sorry, man," and slipped the paper between Will's back and the chair on his way to the counter to order a latte. Gerhardt gave no acknowledgement, although Will would have liked to have some coffee together first. Will wondered why Scott had called, what rules they would be playing by this time. Whatever Scott had in mind, Will would follow. He had missed Scott. He had missed being Gerhardt, the Gerhardt who now took control with practiced finesse, reaching around to scratch his spine and palm the paper.

It read, "Lady in orange sweater at counter. Photo. S or s—no trash. Report in two hours." Gerhardt was to follow her, take her picture, and somehow acquire her signature or a souvenir—something she owned, but not something she'd thrown away. Something that'd have a fingerprint on it. Scott's gig as Ferguson would usually involve taking the next person who came to the counter with a similar demographic—lady in her 30's—but Scott had breezed out the door after a brief nod in the direction of the counter. Will wondered if Scott was playing the game or just playing Will. Spy paranoia—he'd seen that in a movie. Everything became suspect. Will could use that paranoia to add to his characterization of Gerhardt the notion that Ferguson might be a double agent.

When they'd first started playing, Scott had frequently chosen hot girls for Will to track, but Will had insisted that, unlike in the movies, real spies had to blend in. Will nixed the hot chick picks, claiming that it'd be too easy for Scott to flirt with the girl and to acquire the scavenger hunt items and information by colluding with her. Will had cited the Missy Inglebrook incident, during which Scott not only acquired her phone number but used it, and the photo on Scott's phone had shown Missy kissing Scott. The souvenir Scott waved in front of Will's face was a pair of shiny pink panties, but Will suspected Scott had bought those just before reporting back. All Will had been able to come up with was change for a quarter, plucked by a wary cheerleader type from her designer wallet. After that, he'd made Scott pick unremarkable people.

Gerhardt studied the woman at the counter. Long legs in beige slacks. A V-necked sweater, cut lower than he expected. Not orange, as Scott had identified it. A softer color, more the color of orange sherbet. Chin-length hair—probably an expensive cut. Brown, curly. A wedding ring. A watch, nothing flashy. Earrings that had little crystal dangles that got tangled in her hair. A sherbet-colored lipstick was the only noticeable makeup. She looked almost familiar, like a barely remembered first-grade teacher. She fiddled with her purse strap as she waited for her latte. She checked her watch, checked her calendar, checked her lipstick, started out the door, changed her mind, came back in, and went to the ladies' room. When she came out, her hair was different somehow.

Will put on the requisite sunglasses and followed her out of Java Jones and onto the street. He scanned the area for Ferguson and he almost lost the woman in the tangerine sweater when she ducked down the steps into D.C.'s Metro system.

He caught up with her on the platform and managed to get on the same car. The car was crowded for a weekend, and there were no seats. This was good, an excuse to close in. Will grabbed a strap near where the woman had curled her hand around the pole. Up close Will could see that her eyes were dark and she was prettier than he had noticed in the coffee bar.

Anastasia, he decided. Eastern European. The long-term mistress of an ambassador, perhaps an unwitting courier for him. "Darling, give this to Sasha when you see him—a book I promised to lend him." The book would have certain passages or letters marked. Will liked the backstory part of it, liked endowing even the most pedestrian passerby with glamorous motives and connections. Gerhardt, of course, was unimpressed by the glamour or the danger. Gerhardt was cool about everything. Gerhardt pulled out his camera phone calmly and snapped a photo of the woman in profile, against a background of a dozen other riders, all but this woman bearing that half-bored subway rider expression on their faces. She, in contrast, looked keyed up, apprehensive, heightened.

Anastasia got off two stops later. Gerhardt rode the long escalator next to hers, and watched the distinctive sweater turn left at the top of the escalator as he considered and rejected the possibility of pushing past the excruciatingly slow older man just in front of him. He lost sight of Anastasia for a minute, but didn't panic. At the top, he too turned left, scanned the scene coolly, and spotted her half a block away, catching a glimpse of her sweater just before she disappeared into a doorway. Gerhardt sprinted down the block. She wasn't in the dry cleaners or the jewelry store. She must have gone into the restaurant. Lace curtains hung halfway up the windows and frosted glass made patterns above the curtains. Limited visibility. Will could see that the restaurant was small, French, and dark. This posed a problem. It'd be too expensive to eat there, and he'd be out of place and noticeable if he did. He'd have to wait outside. He leaned against the window to consider what to do. Gerhardt took over again. Gerhardt pretended to make a call on his cell phone, turning toward the window as if to shield his ear from street sounds.

Through the breaks in the frosted pattern, he could just make out the woman sitting alone at a small table off to one side, checking her watch and fidgeting with her hair. She was going to meet her contact and was nervous about something. Perhaps Anastasia was beginning to suspect that her ambassador was using her. Will's phone conversation got more animated as Gerhardt inventoried the characteristics of her nervousness: she tucked her stray curls behind her ear and a few minutes later untucked them. She rubbed a crystal earring between her thumb and forefinger. She checked the neckline of her sweater by glancing down, then tugged it up a little. Soon she pulled it down again, and paused with her fingertips resting on the skin in the V. She reached for her cell phone, changed her mind, and put it back in her purse. Suddenly, she looked up and a really wonderful smile lifted her whole face, the kind of smile Gerhardt never stuck around long enough to receive, the kind of smile Ferguson got in the first few minutes.

Will had been so intent on memorizing her gestures that he'd missed the entrance of her dining partner, a tall, well-built man in a dark sweater and expensive jeans. Wavy copper hair. Will could see only his back. After he sat down, he reached across the table to touch Anastasia's cheek. She leaned into his touch. Will worked to adapt his backstory. Perhaps the ambassador had sent Anastasia to seduce this man and thus be in a position to gather information from him. Perhaps she was cheating on her ambassador with this man, and providing him with information as a love gift. Perhaps a lovers' lunch was a cover for them both.

Will figured they'd be there for a long, intimate time, and he could dash in after they left and grab a lipsticked napkin. Meanwhile, he too was hungry. He'd have time to duck down the street to the pop shop for a soda and a candy bar, to fuel the longevity of his surveillance. Will admitted ruefully that Gerhardt wouldn't be eating; he'd be smoking a cigarette and waiting relentlessly for his mark to emerge. Good thing Ferguson wasn't along to comment on this breach of character. Of course, Gerhardt had to have some secrets. Maybe Nestlé's Crunch was one of them. Ah. Of course. Gerhardt was known to leave a telltale candy wrapper as a warning or a signal. He bought the Crunch bar, making sure to use American currency. Will wondered what Scott was doing. He suspected that, for once, his own journey would prove to be juicier than any of Scott's. Will wondered if Scott had even followed someone. Either way, impressing Scott with his own adventure would offer a solid sense of, well, victory. He'd prove himself worthy of the renewed friendship, more interesting than the golden boys of tennis.

Will came back from the pop shop juggling the half-wrapped Crunch bar and a bottle of Coke, the cap of which tumbled into the street. When Will looked up, the sherbet sweater and the navy sweater were leaving the restaurant, and Will tossed the opened soda into an alley and trotted after them. The candy bar he stuffed in his pocket as he slowed behind them. They hadn't stayed for lunch—nobody was getting fed today. Hunger of a different sort. The man pulled Anastasia into a deeply recessed doorway, and Will passed a fervent embrace and the kind of kiss he'd only seen in the movies. He really shouldn't be spying on this, but Will always read to the end of every story, and he couldn't quit now. Besides, he didn't have a souvenir or a signature yet. He considered snapping the kiss but couldn't bring himself to do it. Not even for Scott.

He followed them, noting that although they did not talk on their route, they used every plausible excuse to touch each other—his hand in the small of her back as they got on the subway, his thigh against hers on the seat, a flurry when the lights dimmed momentarily in the car, her blush when he reached across her to pick up the discarded newspaper on the empty seat on the other side. Gerhardt followed them down a quiet street to a handsome brownstone with tall windows and leaded glass flanking the door. On the front stoop, Anastasia turned to the man as he fumbled to unlock the door, and her turning brought her to a clear view of Gerhardt, who was pretending to scan the street numbers, checking the paper Scott had slipped him as if for an address and then using his trusty cell phone as if lost and calling for directions. She looked momentarily puzzled, but by then the door was open and the man in the navy sweater pulled her inside.

Will found a low stone wall a few houses down, and sat in the shade of a big maple to finish his candy bar and wait. He scanned the windows for any movement, humming under his breath, but saw nothing and so had to imagine what came next. He imagined Gerhardt as part of it.

Scenarios. Scott loved creating risk, but Will loved creating scenarios. As the afternoon stretched on, Will went to work creating plausible backstories for Scott's renewed interest in the game. Scenario 1: Scott missed the game, or Ferguson, or both, would not risk his status with his new crowd by being seen with Will, and had just realized he could have both worlds if he and Will each went solo every time. Scenario 2: Scott was using Will to prove some point to his new friends—probably that Will would come when called. There may have been a bet involved. Scenario 3: something serious had changed and now Scott needed Will, but was too proud to let on. Will didn't know much about Scott's family—evidently his mom and stepfather argued a lot, and Scott was home as little as possible. Sometimes he stayed with his dad, but because of his dad's new wife, that didn't seem much better. So . . . Scott needed a place to crash but couldn't reveal his ragged family life to his Stepford teammates. Scenario 4: Scott had been kicked off the tennis team. No. He'd quit the tennis team. Why? The club pro had patted Scott's ass once too often. This, Will felt, was possible. He could test this theory on Monday, at least as far as finding out if Scott was still on the team. He could ask Scott outright, or he could get Gerhardt to ask around.

Will did not ask himself how he felt about each possibility. One of Gerhardt's tenets was that anger is an emotion a spy cannot afford.

Forty-five minutes passed, as did the deadline Scott had set. The ringtone of his phone, a tinny rendition of "Secret Agent Man," startled him. He'd forgotten it was anything but a prop.

Scott. "Gerhardt. Time's up. You've failed your mission." It was not a question.

"Ferguson. Security breach. More info later." That gibberish ought to hold Scott off for a little while. Will was not eager to share this with Scott, despite the bragging rights it might give him. Neither was he willing to leave. He felt complicit in the affair, part of it. Rather than being a danger to this couple, Will felt almost as if he were protecting them, a guardian spirit watching the house. He felt as if he knew Anastasia somehow.

When she emerged, flushed and lovely, and floated down the steps to the sidewalk, Will was fascinated by the change in her gait and manner. She was almost upon him when he realized that he was visible. After all, this wasn't a segment of reality television or a virtual computer game. But he was just a kid in sunglasses sitting on a stone wall daydreaming. That wasn't suspicious.

And yet, she stopped, stared hard at him. Her private smile faded from her features. "Are you following me?" Her voice was rich and husky, not at all like the shrill girls Will knew.

Will shook his head vaguely, not sure what Gerhardt would do or say. He tilted his head a little and tried to come up with something. Gerhardt abandoned him on the spot. This was not Anastasia staring at him but a real woman in an orange sweater, a stranger he knew intimate things about.

"Has my husband sent you to spy on me?" And then, more to herself than to Will, "Of course, you'd say no in either case."

Suddenly he realized what power he had. He was a man of mystery, an unknown quantity, the x in the equation. He had information this woman needed. He was Gerhardt.

"No." Will spoke firmly. "No."

"I saw you in the coffee shop, then on the subway. And now here." She didn't seem frightened, just intent on pinning Will to the wall with her stare. The tables were turning. Will was now the object of scrutiny, the regarded one. He wondered if following her was illegal. They were both on the wrong side of right. She held his gaze. "What's your name?"

"Will . . . Gerhardt." That smoky voice had surprised it out of him.

"Well, Will Gerhardt, why are you following me?"

He wanted to reassure her—he meant her no harm. Surely Gerhardt would have an explanation at the ready. Will just stammered. Finally he said, "Yes. I followed you. On a dare. . . " Will let the rest of the sentence die in the still air. No cover story. Almost the truth. "I'm sorry." And he was. He could feel himself growing younger in her eyes, naïve, unthreatening. He himself didn't know if he was acting. "I won't. . ." I won't tell your husband, I won't tell Scott, I won't tell anyone. Our secret.

She touched his lips with her finger, the sign for silence. He nodded. She looked straight at him for a long minute, and Will realized he was holding his breath. He didn't release it until she took his face in both her hands and brought his forehead to her lips. It felt like a blessing. Then she spun around and hurried toward the Metro stop.

The lipstick on his forehead was his souvenir. Later, he'd make up some other story to go with it. Gerhardt took a picture of his own forehead but did not send it to Ferguson.

Instead he sat back on the stone wall and watched her soft sweater fade down the street. She turned her head back to him just once, and when she saw that he wasn't following, she smiled a small, barely perceptible smile. Something about her was familiar. Will now felt sure he had seen her before. And he knew. She was Scott's father's new wife. Will had seen her once, dropping Scott off at school.

Scott had set him up. Gerhardt focused on the scene at the coffee shop. The understated nod toward the counter: Scott had not been acknowledging the barista; he'd been taking his cool leave of his new stepmother. For the first time since he became part of Will's life, part of Will, Gerhardt had failed him. And Ferguson had betrayed Gerhardt. Betrayal is just another tool, Ferguson might have said. There is no right or wrong, only the goal and the pursuit of the goal. Gerhardt could be trusted to be relentless, to pursue his quarry, to ferret out what Scott suspected but could not himself confirm. Gerhardt doing what Ferguson could not. That felt good. It felt good being valuable to Scott again. Once he was no longer useful, however, would he be retired once more, Scott still the puppetmaster? What would Scott do with the information Gerhardt now had? Would he use it against his father? Against his stepmother? Scott would use it against someone. Knowledge is power, to be used to best advantage. What was Will's best advantage? He was complicit in so many crimes.

And he had promised silence. Gerhardt had not been able to prevent that promise. It had been sealed by her lips on Will's forehead. Perhaps to know and not to tell was another kind of triumph. There had been trespass enough.

Will texted Scott: "Ferguson. Mission aborted. Dissolve cell. Gerhardt dead."

Sam Joyner, *Web Ballet at Antelope Canyon*, photograph

Like a Wolf

You had to admire the shapeless genius of his outfit—
upside-down garbage bag over purple shorts.
Just a slit for his bald head, holes punched
through for his arms, and a drawstring
he could tighten in case of rain.
I made him my pace car, and tried to stay
no more than five or six strides back.

My purpose: not win or place, just finish.
Like the rest of us, he knew that on race day
suffering must brave leg cramps and wind,
angst and winding climbs, and hope
must first be numbered and pinned to your shorts—
in his case, #88. I loved the symmetry
of those eights. Twin infinity signs standing

upright, one chasing the other just as I was chasing
him. At mile eleven, when the sun bled
through red rock hills and I tied my warm-ups
at my waist, and real runners flung
theirs into after-race oblivion, I learned
wisdom. Mr. Hefty tore off his garbage bag,
like the Hulk shredding another Armani suit.

And tossed it high. An updraft caught it,
till it floated above what we were, an undulating
river of huff and wheeze pouring out
of the canyon. Floated—an effigy he ran under,
as if he had escaped himself. Old man nipples
peering out at a new world, he tipped
back his head as if drinking the sky and he howled.

Aeolian

I loved Coleridge's theory instantly: our bodies equal harps
played by the wind, while the melodies that spill

from us copy the rapturous soul singing a broken world.
Aeolian, from Aeolus: whose job was to whisper, to huff,

to push around those floating lakes called clouds, to knock
down towns, to bless desire with musk and breeze,

all without showing his windy face. *Aeolian* — if vowels pass
as windows, then surely this word qualifies as the sunniest

cottage in the OED. My nineteenth summer I indentured
myself to a tract builder named J. Liggins and hardly sang

at all, unless the racket of a Hitachi power nailer counts
as song. Eleven duplexes to plant on a parched hill

that fell away into gullies famous for keggers and skunks.
When I said *aeolian* and looked west into that tangle

of June, I pictured my body, a harp among cheap
wind chimes, waiting for a gust to tear through and make

a melody of my loneliness. At night, fireflies blinked
on till my sadness blinked off. And still I dangled,

like the mannequin some jokester hung from the charred
cottonwood down below that suffered rain and sun

and all manner of bird crap for three joyous weeks
before an officer of the law cut it down. I replayed that aria

of falling, which was silence, and dreamed of the clean
moment when singing ends. We framed all summer, walls

without roofs, walls you could walk through, walls
dreaming of glassed windows, and at lunch wrote love notes

on studs to girlfriends we didn't have, notes
waiting to be trapped behind drywall the way desire

gets trapped in skin. It wasn't till late August, when I
power-nailed my foot to a two-by-four in a closet

haunted by imagined dresses, that I truly turned harp.
Or scream machine. My foot breathed enough fire

for a county, a flame that spiked up my leg and numbed
my left arm. *Aeolian* —what a pulsing smear

of vowels. Holes in an otherwise solid word.
If wounds equal experience, then screaming

for J. Liggins who paid me $5.25 an hour off the books
turned my agony into a bargain. Like us, that nail took

the path of least resistance, through leather and sock,
off my third metatarsal, passing through softer flesh

before anchoring in pine. J. Liggins sawed off the ends
of what bound me to the job, a Boise Cascade #2,

and clumped me down two flights of stairs to his wine-red
pickup. In ER they put me under and later brought

me back, and still the room swam with throbs.
Holes let the outside in, turned the inside out.

Basho counts nine holes (along with a wind-swept
spirit like thin drapery) —seven wrapping the face,

and where the body forks a hidden pair of apertures.
Theologians add five more, but stigmata fail

to measure most of us. Touch me, Jesus said, by which
he meant his wounds. And how should we count

the navel, which fed us through months of fat bliss—
a wound and window that lets us dream ourselves

not healed exactly but as our aches have left us trailing
our mother's singing groans. I think of my friend

Ezekiel Gomez — stabbed seventeen times behind
Bowl-a-rama for swiping someone's hat. One fall day

he typed *The quick brown fox jumped over* . . . . That night
he lay in an alley trying to keep inside and outside apart.

Had Ezekiel been an aeolian harp, think of the octaves,
his gasps buried in the white noise of distant traffic.

In the end he had no more than a handful of hours to sing.
Like Jesus. Touch me, Jesus said, by which he meant

what can't be touched. Soon, soon he would ascend.
If the fingers of his friends believed, maybe their hearts

would follow. They touched their doubts, his blood,
and swallowed. He ate flesh with them, flesh

of this world, honeycomb and fish, to make
one body of their many hungers, to multiply his song.

Touch

Another Sunday and up I go again
for the host, hands folded at my belt,
head down before the cross

and the five marks of Christ
the way I learned thirty years ago,
now just as then looking around

to see who's staying behind—
high-schoolers, fathers with babies—
the lot dull as any Wal-Mart Tuesday

until a woman my age slides back
to let a family pass, ears glittering,
blue jeans awash in stained light

like Linda Olezcjeck's blue jumper
those eighth-grade, girls-in-one-row,
boys-in-another First Friday masses,

Linda's mouth closed through every
hymn and prayer, Linda's hair
wing-crisp from strawberry mousse

that wafted like incense
all the way down our pew
and the purgatory of our adolescence.

Lord, I am not worthy, we said
after we shook our neighbors' hands,
Frankie Wnek licking his palm

before he squeezed our knuckles,
Joey Reynolds tickling the girls
with his middle finger, all of us

with butterflies in our stomachs
those awkward moments
we touched each other

in the days before we'd sit alone
aching to be touched,
Johnny Wurtzel looking for a hand

to pull him back from heroin,
Angel Beach reaching out
for the fathers of her five kids,

Danny Boyer wanting someone
to do something other than tease
his lisp and his weight, finding

only a .22 he pressed to his head
one night on Snake Road in the rain.
Joseph McCook and his dead mom,

me and my long-gone father.
So many of us, so many empty hands.
As I fold and fold again

Christ's body with my tongue,
I look up for the woman
who sent me back to Linda

and the rest, but she's gone
as surely as they are
into whatever they've made

of their lives. Back at the pew
I close my eyes and listen
to myself breathing, a prayer

my Buddhist friend taught me.
I feel the air fill my lungs,
sweep through my chest,

shoulders, arms, fingers,
down my legs to my toes,
feel it fill me until I'm nothing

but air and a softened wafer,
familiar taste of boyhood
that I once again swallow down.

Jen Hoppa, photograph

Oasis Prayers

1904: Beni Abbés, Algeria

I assisted at Mass . . . . His chapel, miserable
corridor on columns, covered with rushes! A board
for altar; for decoration a piece of calico with a
picture of Christ; tin candlesticks; a flattened sardine
tin with two bottles that once held mouthwash,
for cruets and tray!
                                    —*General Hubert Lyautey*

Young Joseph, strong as a palm trunk,
never completes even one chore;
his hands evade. He sings hymns off-key,
begs to be baptized: his only exertions.
I try to convince him that he is free,
he may leave, but he squawks louder,
drowns me out. He fancies his life here,
with Marie, Jean, and me, lodging
in the palm chapel fraternity,
a strange little family.
My first convert (so far, my last),
Marie kneels all day, ancient, blind,
a live statue, a giant tortoise,
Our Lady of the Oasis.

Jean creeps behind me, first afraid,
now curious; ready for chores,
I think, and ripe for God. He stares,
bites his nails as I serve wine
and bread to the line of soldiers,
to the commandant and his aide.
I tell my little family
that freeing and naming them
isn't enough. We must pray for francs,
for the thousands to be freed; pray
that fetters unfasten, that Europe
intervenes, that my purse fattens,
that I might make more purchases;

pray that money comes from the gifts
of my good cousin and sister,
from the officers at the fort,
and from the dole of the White Fathers,
my patrons, the Missionaries
of Our Lady of Africa.
I tell them, but Marie, Joseph,
and Jean only nod at my babble,
perplexed by most of my words.
I am a novice of all these
desert tongues. Language cloisters me.
We must draw figures in the sand,
or gesture. Our hands become birds,
pulling new shapes from the air.

Gerald Cournoyer, detail from *Bleak Winter*, acrylic on canvas

Words for Flesh

1906: Tamanrasset, Hoggar, Algeria

I cannot sketch the Tuareg. I am too slow to catch
the departing backs of men on camels, gone in a flash,
racing for pasture and trade. And if I studied
the warbling women who tend goats all day and dance
slack-breasted when the sun bleeds the black crags red,
I would have to pluck the lust from my eyes. The women
strum toothing-stones and one-stringed violins, stretch
hides over kettles, bang them for drums. If I am careless,
I find myself humming their tunes instead of the psalms.
But there are other ways to learn the Tuareg people.
I assemble a grammar, a dictionary; I translate
Tuareg poems, the gospels. My first words include:
bowl, and *milk*, and *moon*, *star*, *eye*, and *fire*, and *ash*.
Dassine rules the Tuaregs when her cousin rides away.
Pale, lithe, brown-eyed, she shares with the other women
my sewing notions, my health advice and medicines.
I have her ear. I trade words, from their language
to mine, and back again. My knowledge at its end,
I trip over Tifinagh script. Her warm hand guides
my hand. I try, try, smudge the words I fail to shape.

Wagoneering

All us kids had them—
Red-painted and squeaky-voiced—
banged and busted and bumped. The rust
even gleamed in certain angles of light.

Character (or something equally parental)
was what our parents called it.
We called it rust, ferruginous grit
dusting denimed behinds.

Summers we played under the sign of the axle
that turned clockwise on zodiacs of sky-high thoughts:
Green Thumb, Coaster, Radio Flyer.
Our wagons were genie lamps, magic wands.

From mine I pulled daylight by the handle
up the down hills of Kentucky yards,
the quest spinning in spokes, the child
in me old with my love affair for wheels.

Already I was revising, editing dead ends
to prairies, mud holes to rivers gone rough,
their currents shifting in foamy eyes.
At the ford I crossed on rubbery joints

scanning the here to there of this and that,
ancestor-stepping, west anywhere I pleased.
The tracks I followed went slantwise
down different roads. The ones behind me

circled what I carried.
Something rumbled on the radius.
Something else clanked and clamored
on the hairpin turn.

I moved deeper into wilderness
steely on tire-charmed legs,

a blackbird on some far branch
something dangerous, dangerous for sure—

a bobcat, a bushwhacker, maybe an Indian.
I lay low inside my wagon's red ribs,
the saga axle-high hanging
from my pockets, dirty on my knees.

Carol Bierer, pencil drawing

Transphysical

How do I enter her story? I know only dust
devils and feathers to compare, an heirloom music
box missing several pins,

the motions of her pleated
skirt, a prairie as ocean for chorus; not one wholly
discrete from the others.

I know from where I stand,
a lid in the scene seems to lift when she floats
daily by the tides of wheat—a mirror

of pastures passing behind me,
her body displacing my presence—
my mind captive to a shimmer and strut

her body can't stop, her hips and sway singing
metal tines inside. She always follows
this gear-work logic faster,

frets the spring unwound could play her
melody broken as silver-backed glass for our fault-
lined reality—our fall-out reason found

in all the flickering lamps of this tavern-ridden town.
I aspire to offer sweet words, a metaphor in birds—
my thoughts are flocks flown in whichever

weather she conjures. My migratory mindset of bombshell
descent abruptly suspends
and ascends her wicked little whirlwind.

My thoughts are flocks flung at the ether
or plummet and thump
the ground as my pulse.

Each other's fingers dovetail our ribs,
the particular pelvic
augury of song.

Pants

How inhuman they appear
this moment,
their loony ductwork rising to the illogical crotch,
the absurd absurd plurality of them.

The inseam alone is an abomination,
the zipper rippling, millipedal. Impossible
to believe anyone
ever ever cooked such things up.

Take the yodel,
or the Elizabethan ruff accordioned about a courtier's neck
like a poodle-cut.
Oddities no more preposterous than this platypus

of apparel, emerging
just now
from the primordial soup of the clothes pile
onto the stark surface of awareness.

For two full minutes I *tsk* at the creation
of the belt loop, the undeserved
demise of the toga,
the singular goofiness of cuffs.

❊

And we who go into them,
feet first
each morning, sitting on the edge of the bed,
or stooped

to ladle the paraphernalia
of our sexes into the bladderchamber dangling
just there
about the shins,

we who furrow
our legs into their legs,
fork ourselves over to their keeping
down to the last follicle,

are we not too
silly silly creatures proliferating in our corduroys,
swaddled and monstrous and
perfectly crazy for the Cha-Cha.

Knee as Nostalgia

As history, it is a sad horse
in a sad pasture nibbling the sad sugar
from the palm of years gone by.

As diplomat, middleman, lugubrious. True
the decades merge, engage, but always with the same outcome.
The knee was made to bend in one direction only.

As old ball bearing, rolling and lubricated with reminiscence,
it is your uncle, the one who seems to have been old always.
As Lon Chaney, it remembers a good 700 faces.

With patience it can be brought to perform,
to jump and jab like a cupped bird, like the heart
of a cupped bird.

It doesn't really groan, maybe wheeze a little.
It can be flexed and make rifle sounds and go bald,
then withdraw, lie stiff and straight

with a forlorn tremor of its thick walnut eyelid
on which reside the worry wrinkles
of the best minds of its generation.

Mockingbirds, or Other Beings of Flight

You were so disappointed in me.

In my heart each night
I worry there will be no dreams
worth telling you in the morning.

I worry there will be only
my failure as I remember
two birds caught in one rhythm
that flew into the hallway
outside Gavrilo Princip's cell
and barracks where I still
feared the sound of the train's clacking

and that then suddenly circled out
into the graveled yard and back in,
not at first believing misery
could exist so many decades later,
only to fly out again, finally,
to a sky that was blue and great—

two birds with the good
sense to leave me.

I want to ask you why
you love me.

Please.

It's an honest question.

What I Learned from Birds

was not how to sing, swoop, or fly.

These birds had fallen from a tree in a parking lot near a wall
      covered so thick with ivy that if I pressed
            up against it, seven years would disappear.

Treasure or tragedy, a moment would decide. Blood bouldered through
      my veins, gathered its greater red as I sprinted for help:
            my instinct already given its volume.

Mother and I inspected. The nest, no bigger than the bowl
      I could make with my hands, had landed up,
            a cradle to a small group of birds only moments old.

Next to it, a mother with a fractured skull, her feathers clotted
      on the concrete with a blackened glue of blood
            so that when the wind blew, her wings would catch in it,

as if about to lift. I learned that not all flapping wings could fly.

We took the birds to a box that once closed over my shoes,
      lined with rags, leaves, and sticks. The front porch housed
            the live scent of their bodies—not quite birds—

but spongy machines. They glowed blue veins and their tiny
      one-hundred-beats-per-minute hearts punched against their paper breasts.
            After a whole day of studying them—
                little hooks the shape of an inner ear—

I learned what I looked like in my mother's womb.

Their eyes bulged milky globes, hard to discern open
      from unopened, dead eyes from seeing eyes. But after
          three straight days and four pairs of dead eyes,

I learned the difference, could sense the second life went out

the way I could pinpoint the very revolution that "Mean Mr. Mustard"
      became "Polythene Pam" on the record player. And so I named them.
          The third one had wrenched into his silver hammer

by morning and I learned that two can be a great number.

When it was just Polythene left after a single week

I learned how far one is from two. I learned that seven days is an eternity
    because it takes that little before a bird's wings tell it to fly.

And when I saw Polythene living out of a box again
      years later, I did not recognize her.
          In trying to study her from across the street

I learned how years can sharpen a body out of its gender

so she was no longer a woman but vines of ivy leaf
      and gears of a gritty machine. Her hair clotted together in soot
          and when wind caught in the clumps, it was as if
             knotted birds
               were lifting
                   from her ears.

The distance, I learned, between one place and another, just seconds.

Lightning Tree

Lightning planted
a birch tree
upsidedown.
The white tree grew whiter,
firmly rooted
in the clouds.

The branches dusted
the forest floor
so the sky
could see its reflection.
The birch flew away
in a snowstorm
with others of its kind.

From the collection of the Editor, photograph

Transcription of an Accident

I knew you
Before twilight birds chortled blackness
     And seven lullabies were staggered inconsequentially
I knew you
Before the motorcycle
Before Tantalus stole the bottle
     And we drank the thoughts of gods
I did not know you, though,
After the cannonball into ice water,
     The well-whiskey flow
     Like Tahquamenon whirling
     A froth of words.
The engine not purring or coughing or roaring
But for your hands to weaken the throttle's resolve
The foam still clinging to our breath.

I knew you
Where cherry baums
     Exploded in black feathered wings
     And saw with one eye
     Angels hybridize with humans
I knew you
In the mountain pass
Between antiquity
     And antediluvian

I knew,
Where I grasped up at the sky
In the black heat
Before valleys
Caressed letters
Only the deaf could know,
I did not know you, then,
Save for the stillness of your thighs,
Between the flickers of tomorrow,
The beeping and inconsistent whiteness,
Counting upward until time stopped, and there,

The everything and nothing.
Tea-cup images
Flocks of bones rolling and tumbling,
The rage of birdsong, and the ground.

Lot 4726

I.
The bitten apple
When it is not gilded
Nor poisoned
Nor bearing the fine imprint
Of serpentine scales

Tastes of the farmhouse
Before grandma started calling
Me by my father's name,
As if thirty years
Had been condensed
In a single fruiting body.

II.
It was after
Biting the crab apple
She had thrown at me
While we were both seventeen
And juice slipped
Between lips

New seeds
Were planted in rings
Around roots
In the backyard.

III.
If it was picked
After the first frost
And has been rinsed
Before being peeled,
The apple, when bitten,

Smells like the dirt after a hard rain
When all the worms surface
For fear of drowning,
And we splash in the puddles
Hoping one day to have a vessel.

IV.
When the snow
Is melting and the
Bitten apple leaves
A sticker bearing the name of a place
More than halfway around the world
Between the tooth that never
Ended up straight and
The one that got knocked out
A few weeks after the braces
Came off,

Then, it is enough,
For now.

Missing

splinters of shagbark hickory, ascent of ivy
on catalpa, alder, elm, layering memory

upon memory — the sycamore shedding skin
persistent in the work of letting go —

the black walnut, gingko, burr oak
dropping wings and mottled fruit —

crowns, trunks, limbs, stark shadows
cast on moonlit snow erased —

the forest along Old Plank Road
that flourished as long as I can remember —

gone, bark, pith, core, in one day two acres,
hundreds of trees severed to stumps,

roots upended, their silhouettes
etched against the sky. If I'd known,

I would have risked trespassing
that glory field, listened to warbler,

hawk, spotted owl cry one last time.
I could have sung hosannas for leaf and bough,

for the faith of saplings. It was one place left
in the city, a reprieve from traffic rush

where once I watched deer cross
at dusk, dancers leaping into darkness.

Photo of a Caterpillar

Cimbex femorata

Her plump body curls, pale green spiral,
black ink spots on hairless flesh,

bare as gingko branches in winter,
as a needy heart. She looks like she crawled

from an ancient urn, camellia petals,
or cherry blossoms in Arakwa.

She's plunged headlong across
our desktop from Siberia's Lake Baikal

where it isn't the frigid world we imagined,
but summer with finch wings, daffodils,

a background unlikely as the hideaway
Ferlinghetti kept in Rainbow Canyon,

his cabin shrouded in fog hanging
over hairpin curves that seem to fall

into the sea, on the brink, insatiable
craving, like a wingless larva latched

to a bamboo twig, and she is
an Asian watercolor, little ambassador

waiting to transform, like the chasms
we cross blind as the Snake River

rushing where it must, every turn
unknowable as the path of a whooping crane

on the verge of extinction. How determined
she is, her silky skin glistening,

and we still teeter on the edge
between risk and want.

Paternal Parallax

He taught me about symbiosis,
the caterpillar's harmony with trees.

And there were other moments
of extraordinary kindness.

Once, I shrugged off his hug in a cafe
and outburst followed. Anger then

stone. For months I became
a ghost town, disordered, blown open.

On Sundays I'd slip
poems under his door like grenades,

make him sit through the war
the way I did.

Larisa Leonova, photograph

After Your Harsh Words

The horizon swallows the sun —
belly first. The mind

goes like the sea
it's out on. Fingers, suddenly wild

and foreign, trace the ridge of a brow
searching for meaning. Even Braille

fails to translate. Jaws open like giant
gates, where something consumes me.

Somewhere there must be song
fluted and rising. But here

in the house of what is
I am undone by simple things, the walls

in all their hollowness, a bit of crumb
carelessly swept

under the fridge, the uncaught tongue
slipping.

Nocturne: Next Room

Last night, only ten blocks from where we slept, a pursuit before
        the destined crash
jarred sleeping families awake, the accordion-coiled metal

        from each car
landing upturned on cross-street sidewalks. And when I say we,
        I mean you—always

awake I seem these days, predicting steel-toes bluntly hammering
        our front and back
doors, the cats below us knocking a space-heater into curtains,

        the collective building's
sleep too deep to awaken from the fire. It's as if the cold, depriving
        moisture from our skin,

forebodes our future withering, the sirens and their spinning mirrors
        cracking and exploding
under the weight of it all. What happens when we choose not

        to be rescued? Far gone
now, I'm on the balcony listening: how many blocks away, how many
        involved, if anyone

has been saved. And as I wait for sleep, hear your breathing
        in the next room
at dawn, I'm afraid the sky will not change, endlessly echoing this night.

Nocturne: Newark, NJ

Spools of smoke uncoil from refinery
after steadfast refinery — I cannot bear

mango, milk thickened with egg, your arm
stirring endlessly. Like you, Mother,

I am hungry always. But what can you
know of loneliness? You are not the empty

corner dusk pours through, its windows divided
by light. You are not the incantations of palms

pressed over eyes the color of bruises — in that photo,
your curls reel across the pillow — cheek to cotton,

cotton to collarbone — like you, Mother, I have fallen
asleep dreaming overcrowded graveyards. Can you be

that young girl and the weeping mother whisking milk
into cream? Can this face in the dark window be mine?

Wherever You Are

> . . . For sadness, we prescribe a
> friend. For death a friend. Run
> to meet us on the road.
>
> —*Rumi*

I want to tell you I can't figure out
how I've ended up here for months
in a small rain forest cabin above
this mountain stream. Quiet all summer.
And now with the first winter downpour suddenly
pounding the roof and the whole living mountain —
flailing the limbs of the banyan tree
near my window, the stream floods to a surging
roar — rising twenty feet in no time
a fierce widening curve — rolling spume and
debris down slope — taking the showy haleconia.
The uprooted hau tree — gone.
Even the stalky purple ginger on the highest bank
that a day ago waved its sundrenched color in the air —.
The wind strikes the wild bamboo
against the wall near my bed.
And night coming on fast. The terror of
the natural world, stronger than any intention
and moving at its own relentless speed.
Hard as I try, I never had eyes for the future
and now only for this terrible undoing and for
the completely present and unseen world.
I stay this long to witness the necessity of
carnage, another reminder that nothing is ours
for long. I wish you could have seen, though,
the wild Night Heron all summer long —
his beautiful persistence at the edge of the water
and how easily he slipped into the fearless dark.
I want to tell you, friend, the road is not so far.
And I am on my way!

ROBERT GRUNST

Bronzy Incas

Meantime we will be making desultory
trips around the plaza.
— *E-mail from our daughters at Sanare, Venezuela*

And you will be *searching perhaps for chocolate,*
you write, *in various*

shops. Of the *large brown hummingbirds,*
you say, *they nest*
         in perfect

cups of moss. Sometimes my eyes say
nothing here

belongs to us. It's the computer screen.
It's early afternoon.

The words are strange —
the words are
        out of place.

But I don't know what place I mean —
flour, sugar, yeast,

panadería, where you say you buy
these things.

It's your *desultory trips around the plaza*'ve
thrown me off, I guess,

trying to imagine you just now from here:
your field station
        in *Yacambu,*

spotted barbtails'

nests, 120 true cloud forest epiphytes, yellow
warblers on a fence,
        the straggly

dogs and cars. I love the cars! I know your r
is meant to be a

t. Though maybe not. *Male fruit crows flare
out bright red throats
                              in their displays,*

you say. *They produce a loud bombing sound.
They nest along the river.*

Maybe it's *booming* that you mean.

I think you must remember winds booming
above the uncapped

cistern in Iowa City—Davenport St.—when you
were five, and I lowered

you both down, then pulled
you back again;

there was a tornado there just last week
that wrecked St.

Patrick's Church. Razed the green steeple.
Peeled off the roof.

The spotted barbtails' nests are funnels
of fiber and mud.

You write of *Blood-eared parakeets. . . .*

*The Black-faced
                         ant thrushes'*

*songs sound like a yodel falling near
then spinning off.*

They're not true thrushes though. Anti-
thrushes, I can't help but

think, thinking of this twisting; this unraveling—
morels:
> *We'll miss another*

Minnesota spring   Wood

creepers big curved-billed foragers   Egg-
plants
> *last year near*
>> *Bolinas*

Bull kelp I miss you *Cooper's hawk*

Palomarin

> You say there is

a recipe we can try after we arrive.

Three more weeks: our flight will land well after dark.

Meanwhile our clocks are only one hour
apart,

and I've been thinking of the white-faced capuchins
you've described,
> *clattering through the canopy,*

stealing the eggs of Band-tailed guans.

They are omnivorous, I've read, the capuchins:
One source says, *They have*
> *complex*
>> *social lives.*

On their heads they have a tuft of hair
reminiscent of

the cowl or capuche worn by Franciscan monks.

We will hire a taxi.
> From Barquisimeto it's

*fifty kilometers and all but seven
wind and climb.*

We'll meet you in the plaza.

                    Plaza Bolívar.

Your capuchins. The liberator cast in bronze.
History's
              place is

every place and spins and importunes
us.

Of the guans, you say, *They have red dewlaps.
They're turkey-like.*

                    Their eggs are white.

There is no sound like the sound of guan shell grinding
between
              a monkey's teeth — the sucking
                                        down

of albumen and yolk.

Down the street outside this office a siren's screaming.
Cars, a bus, are pulling over

to the curbs.

*Sometimes we hear shots. Hunters cut through
our plots,* you write. *They kill*

the monkeys, capyberas too.

They carry machetes. They have a gun,
a shell or two.

Poaching is their way of life. They have no time for
birds. They don't need GPS.

They know exactly what they can get in trade for fifteen
pounds of wild meat.

Cross

I buy clay figurines you need to sell—
been shelling out since you approached last May
beneath La Cruz: lizards, sheep, a snake,
wild bird with fish caught in its mouth, that fell

when you ran off; it's not the first to break.
When out of glaze, it's chicle for a cent
or two cents for a solo cigarette.
Each day, I smoke an Alas for your sake.

But when I go, Chavito, I'll be done
with one shrewd smile. Only a fool collects
a city of clay beasts, a cloying brand

of gum, blows smoke in hope of changing luck.
Only a fool throws coins against the wreck.
I hoard a tail, a wing, a mouth, a hand.

My Dress Hangs There

In southern Mexico, the rainy season
is a woman, the amber life-in-death
of summer, where I greenly catch my breath.
The mist transforms; no utterance is common.

Returning North in winter, I am back:
our ordered world, typed on a finite sky,
bootprints on snow. Are green visions mine,
so fragile that they chip when I unpack?

I think of Frida—*My Dress Hangs There*
between two countries, of Persephone,
who wouldn't face the winter in despair.
For Hades, she'd stow a pomegranate seed.

For you, I tell what happens when I roam,
how trespassing the border brings me home.

Sam Joyner, photograph

The Man in the Barrel

The man going over Niagara Falls in the barrel
changed his mind halfway down
and nothing was ever the same again in the theater
showing the newsreel of his barrel—hardly more than a black
smudge in the grainy black and white photograph
the stopped film became. It was hell getting the man out of the barrel.

People remarked for years that a mind should never be changed
in the midst of such an eventful undertaking.
And this was impressed upon the next generation of children
whose minds were never changed, not once,
after they decided something.

The man who changed his mind in the barrel
never changed it again. Once removed from the barrel he lived
an obscure life unable to convince anyone
that changing his mind was more important than completing the ride
over the falls. After all, he argued,
many had ridden barrels and even other contraptions over the falls
but no one had effectively changed his mind
in the middle of the fall.

You have no idea, he would argue to those who remembered him,
what it took to change the mind
after the barrel had ceased buoyancy and plummeted.
You try it, he would say. Try stopping
everything that shifts you into the next moment—especially if
you chose that moment—try pitting your own
lump of gray matter against all the known physical forces propelling
you pell-mell toward the one thing you most desired
above everything else in the world.

Late November New Lake Ontario

First snow, and the apple crop is in.
Diego and Manuel take their orchard songs
back home to Florida.
Blue-gray sky; curled brown leaves
fall and fly for weeks.

All morning we sing and bake bread,
read until dusk, pray in the dark.

Nightshade and blackberry, wild rose, osier and vetch,
foxes under the stone wall, mice in the granary,
here and there an unpicked Jonathan or Empire
inviting the lips of deer —
everything slowed in snow, waiting.

Sometimes It Is Unclear

Sometimes it is unclear where
the radiance
of mist begins
about a lake

in the dark moist foliage
or smoking
through black symphonic
trees, sliding

stone to stone
in a heavy understanding
the radiance begins
wrapping trees

birds carrying it
and its flowers that
you loved
for their secret

withheld
and thick whiteness
like the sky
full with moon

all you accept you
will receive
when the white life
white macula leaves

the bad wife

There is no answer to what comes next, no sign to announce *keep this secret*. The glass of wine. The evening. You are difficult: holding the cool glance one moment longer than appropriate, as you do all things.

But all things evolve, and quickly: quartz to dust, the gnaw of a questioning mark, the crush of an infant star. Tomorrow, I'll be a galaxy of trumpets. Or a world of little things you've lost or drunk in one long drink. (What you do not want.)

But what do I know? A comet passes, unnoticed, and the bad wife strays deep into the forest, to the thorny belly of tall trees. You are the scratch I've gotten there: scarlet in the yellow scrape of leaves.

From the collection of the Editor, photograph

The Untranslated Poem

Let the Emperor take a bath in the hot spring with
his consort, the most prized one of them all, who
is languid, beyond compare, custard-flesh flaunting,
her moonface still flush from the water-heat.

Let her sit at the boudoir combing her hair like she's
bowing a cello, and let one of her breasts tumble
out like a rabbit, bare. Let him approach, reach for
that nipple, and call it a stud of jade in a quatrain.

Let her looks topple the Dynasty. You the river
merchant's wife wait, yellowing with
October, still pacing the void
as far as Cho-fu-sa.

Spherical Lightning

She alone saw it drift in;
the childless aunt was in the
kitchen, the men out in the field.
The child alone watched the bright ball
bound in silently from the open window like a
question (a curt "would you?" or "and if
it *were?*" that she could have scooped up
with both hands), touching nothing, and
back through the two osmanthus
trees out front.

       What she remembers
most was the subjunctive mood of the
whole thing, as if wonderment was itself
amulet. The hush was nothing like the
Taoist priests hired afterwards to exorcise
the intact house, nothing like knowing,
years later, that ploughmen got struck dead
in the fields. Thunderstorms, they said,
shaking heads, and after each burial was the
familiar shuffle: villagers declaiming all
at once, to say what sorrow the dead
must've had coming, then the whisperings:
speculations of reprehensible acts, possibly,
unbeknownst to the yet living, before the bolt hit.

Lord of Dust

He
has
grown
huge in
his only
room, wrapped
in a web built to
look like just some
careless dust, his fly-high
apartment inside, efficiency
in the corner. I get a bit of
a bite of fear discovering him so
close, however much I quickly play
the worldly one, eating my sandwich
while I study the guy-lines holding his
home together, the way his gray hidey-hole
curls upwards and back like some undertaker's
happy cornucopia, corpses dangling. We are much alike,
discarding our successes once the juice has been sucked out.
He won't move while I'm watching, betting he'll go unnoticed,
all eyes on the insensate world, this purveyor of final meals.

By the Poppy

He is a worthless old sot,
nibbling cheap figs
and herding his sheep
from pasture to pasture,

but he is warm in the winter,
dry in the rain,
and full when the picky
eater starves.

He is the King of sheep
here and in Asia.

And no one in his kingdom
is in the mood for revolt.

It makes no difference
what clothes he wears
or how fat his
wallet is or is not.

The poppy flower is red
and the young shoot is green

and that has nothing
to do with the value

of a poppy.

This set of poems are recreated, fictionalized translations of the work of Archilochus, a Greek poet of the 7th Century BCE, derived from existing fragments of his poems or based on what is known of the poet's life.

Stitching the Poem

When Odysseus sailed into the seas of my mind
I knew that this was a gift from Kalliope.
Odysseus is our best chance to pervert the rule of morons.

I almost made Achilles a man when he wept with Priam.
I did manage to make Hector an adult, loving his wife,
defending his country, dying when he must,
and now and then even Patroclus had a moment
of humanity and compassion, but
it just pisses me off, letting the nobility win
with their shit-ass epics about false bravado,
idiotic nationalism, and their infantile sense of honor.
I tried to influence the Sons of Homer
by writing those bits of the epic that are thinly
disguised propaganda to the contrary, portraying
love and empathy and maturity and thought —
including the killing of Thersites and the death of Hector.

So I gathered all the stories of Odysseus' return,
and the nostos of the other heroes,
and wrote a fantasy of gods and men,
included all the places and wonders I have seen,
with a hero who was wise, grown up and eager to live,
who turns down immortality for the sake of remaining
a mortal human — a man who knows how to love.

Odysseus sings in my veins,
travels in my ships, wins all my battles,
swings his sword, uses his shield
and then picks up the lyre and sings about the home
he will always be voyaging toward.

I will take the poems to the Daughters of Homer,
to young Erinna, and let a woman stitch the hexameters into Epic,
plaster it with Homer's name and turn it loose
on the world, an anodyne for the poisons in the Iliad
and the half-wit minds of the aristocracy.

No one will know our names, but who knows if
some far-descended son of ours, some suffering poet,
may live a better life because we told the truth.

The hour is late and the war with the Naxians looms like some
idiotic and unavoidable storm on the horizon — come what will,
fight we must, and die if we have run out of choice.

To hell with Kings and heroes —

It is time for wine.

From the collection of the Editor, photograph

Storm Coming

It is the dark cold before the dawn.
It is the fear that comes true
when you least expect it,
when it's too late
to do a damn thing about it.

Now the waves have gone fierce and choppy.
The waves are trying
to pull down the stars.

I elbow Glaukos and nod out to sea.
He looks out, frowns and nods back.

It is enough that our stomachs churn
muddy water and flash floods
thinking about wars and battles
and death and dying
and that army of better men
we face tomorrow.

"Nothing to worry about—
We'll probably drown in that
pot of boiling waves
before we even get across."

The waves are reaching for the stars
and can't seem to make up their mind
on a common direction,
bashing against one another
and crashing against the cliffs of Gyrae.
The waves look mean enough to
turn the best made boat to kindling.

Above the cliff there is an army
that does not have to cross the waves.
Above the cliff there is an army
that is eating a hearty breakfast
with calm stomachs.

Above the cliff the moonlit cloud
has turned to coal and ash,
rumbling thunder
and thrashing rain.

Above the cliffs of Gyrae
the storm reaches for our throats
and calls each man by name.

Manly Johnson, photograph

Amber as the Rock of Sisyphus

The deeper I got into amber
the more I saw of my life —
burrowing in I catapulted
outward, I could almost sit on the moon
watching the patterns,
the great concerns, the years.

It's only when I'm almost gone that
all this will become clearer.

Again I entered amber
and tried, for a day, or a week,
to give up everything else, which

takes revenge, at the very least
in your dreams. To get anything clear as sight
you have to give up on another sense, which
                has a life of its own —
the way you pay your rent
has fangs. The words of a friend
have temperature. What makes you comfortable
     has everything.
The deeper I got into amber the more
 I was guilty of being human.
And I couldn't comprehend the light
    I lived in, or
             the light in the stone.

A gemstone borrows its light.

And our stone, alive in darkness?

What name do I give to the
match-keepers beneath the ground
  where we are buried?
     Espiritus alcohol spirochete virtues
      Alpha and Omega
   Pluck.

What name to the oxygen
that can't, but does, survive there,
  to feed the imminent light?   ~~*Memory-breath*~~
     Thought-breath.
What name to the matches,
their number unlimited?
       ~~*A memory of ferns, the collective un-, our holy remains*~~
      Finders-keepers.

What name to the precious stone unearthed?

     Amen.

Matches secure in my pocket, I waited
    for the wee hours:

  Where there's death, there's light.

I dream of giving

I tied a knot in my mother's hair.
      She was not there.
Her eyes loose in airless air.
I made her small, tied a ribbon in her
      child's hair.
She smiled. And still was
              not there

but in Rilke's castle, combing her hair;
      like a mirror
he turned and turned toward her.
          I told her
I'm here—my echo struck amber,
         up, up a wide stair
and both turned—O this earthen light bared
     their
eyes, their eternal stare
         paling where
it was struck blind, and my mother's hair
flew into a sticky black rage, no,   despair.

Hush, I re-tied the braid and the bows, there
      now, hear
me, Mama, I'll leave you in tenderer
hands, and softly turning away, they disappeared

      hand in hand, up there

Kazatzke

Young man dance Kazatzke, at wedding parties in rented ballrooms at Hotel
  Statler Westbrook Sheraton, in auditorium vestry rooms at Temple
  Sinai Emanuel Beth Zion, carry on tradition, carry generations on
  your back, you Stephen Dedalus, you Yahrtzeit Candle you

Dance Kazatzke, folded arms, acrobatic squat and kick, mettle-testing squat
  and jump, keep your balance, prove your manhood once and for all,
  you rite of passage, you Sisyphus, you condor in the wind you

Dance Kazatzke, show up all those goyim/Cossacks, all those frowning
  alte-kockers, all those indifferent women, all those laughing patronizing
  so-called friends, show them what you're made of, what you can do,
  you Raskolnikov, you revolution journal you

Young man dance Kazatzke, testify that you were born to power which is
  beauty, born to hit a homer, score a touchdown, sink a basket at the
  buzzer, born to do great things, to live triumphant, you Argonaut, you
  golden boy you

Dance Kazatzke, because you're such a lover, such a gash man, let the
  world know you're free-wheeling, no one can tell you what
  to do, let them know you love that you are loved, you Casanova Romeo
  you arrow in your heel you

Dance Kazatzke, dance away the sorrows of your blood's oppressive
  yesterdays, you're the spirit of regeneration, you're living in the
  moment, living magnitudes, you Elie Wiesel holocaust survivor, you
  war memorial wailing wall you

Young man dance Kazatzke, dance to Ivy-Leaguer artificial faux-naïve
  phony old-world Klezmer music, dance to fiddle sax and drums in
  Buffalo with memories nostalgic sweet and sad, you Wandering Jew
  Tom Sawyer Gulliver, you time-discolored ship of fools you

Dance Kazatzke, dance ecstatic, virile, proud to the Tommy Dorsey band
  playing *And The Angels Sing*, and the Kazatzke
  trumpet solo electrifying unforgettable, and everywhere's aurora
  borealis rainbow autumn colors summer lakes and beaches resurrection
  spring and brave and epic winter all at once, you Dionysius drunken
  angel Ziggy Elman, you, lion of perpetuation you

Dinner With Foreigners

Everything black
on the ride down
no heat, ice
on the windows three
centimeters thick,
the moon
couldn't get through
just the click click
swaying against the tracks
dark consonants beating
into the stiff snow

After the hugs
greetings you have carefully
memorized they try
Clint Eastwood, all
they know of English
and you know
no movies in their language

you jerk phrases out
like the sweater
you wanted on the train
in the middle of your bag
(your hands stiffening
in the dark cabin)
you got pants, then bra
instead: *Thanks*
for invited you
here. The chicken
tastes pretty.

Conversation clatters on;
you remember
craning your ears
upwards as a child
toward the dark blur

of adult chatter
trying to smile
at the right moments
click click
swaying against the tracks

Another round of vodka.
One man, an actor.
begins to tell a story
with his hands
the noises of animals,
trains and buses,
you think you understand.
His name is Niko.
You try it now,
just like a game
you played as a girl:

a match flickers
in front of each face
leaning forward
a string of bright bulbs,
personalities —
you have a personality,
rescued
from the cold dark
cabin of your childhood.

The ride home is ice-free,
lights dim and warm
enough to doze (drunk)
against the soothing
click click click that means
you are moving forward
and when you remember
the night you remember
how it took place
entirely in your language,
whatever that was.

Chekhov in Brighton Beach

Semyon woke up to the sound of the key in the lock of the entrance door. Essy came in from the street, tired and chilled. Two packs of frozen dumplings weighed down her knit-string shopping bag.

Semyon sat reclining in an armchair and looked pointlessly at his wife. He was about to get up and help her to take off her coat, but he couldn't move. He had come from the Leningrad City Theatre terribly tired and hadn't realized he had dozed off.

"You know what, little Essy," he said, muffling his voice, "maybe you're right after all. Nothing can be done. Let's get the hell out of this country!"

"Thank God, finally!" Essy said vigorously, but her voice broke. Semyon glowered at his wife. Beyond the window, Moika Avenue rustled with wet tires; streams of afternoon sunlight that managed to make their way through a veil of clouds made puddles gleam.

This was not the first time they had talked about emigrating from Russia. Essy had kept the official invitation from seventy-two-year-old Naum, her uncle on her father's side, in their dresser, under a pile of bedclothes, for a long time. Naum had already lived a few years in New York, in the Bronx, north of Manhattan. He wrote that all was well with him and that, though he survived on welfare, it was enough for a modest living. The only true shortage for him was that of his loved ones.

"What will I do there, Essy?" Semyon would ask his wife.

"You're an actor, Syoma, a damn good actor. And you know it. Was there a single review that didn't take note of your work?"

"What are you talking about, Essy? What kind of future could an actor who doesn't speak English possibly have in America?"

"Well, you'll find something."

"There you go—something! I'm a Russian actor, you understand, Russian!"

"And what kind of future do you have here, in this swamp of a country, ah? No air to breathe. Then again, you're a Russian actor, all right—but you're a Jew."

"What's Jewish about me? Do I visit a synagogue or read a

Jewish book? In Hebrew or Yiddish? What do I know about Jewish history and culture? Nothing! I read some Sholom Aleichem in Russian translation in my youth. That's about it."

"As if it makes any difference to them!"

Essy's remark touched a raw nerve. He had become angry and left the room, slamming the door. Indeed, he felt uncomfortable with the fact that he, an actor in a Russian theatre, was Jewish. He tried to hide it whenever he could. When introducing himself to new people with his first name and his patronymic, as customary in Russia, he Russified both of them, calling himself Semyon Mikhailovich, instead of Samuil Moiseevich, as his identification papers had it. It was silly, of course, for everyone knew that his surname was Spielman.

The decision to give in to his wife's pleadings to leave Russia wasn't an easy one. It came in despair, a deep sense of hopelessness that dulled his feelings and made him indifferent to his fate.

The last straw had been the casting of a new play. Again he got nothing. The theatre was big and prestigious, and the director was known all over the country, but there just weren't enough parts for everybody in the huge troupe—over fifty actors! Each time he was given even a small part, it was a cause for a celebration.

Time spent without acting was torture to him. Prolonged idleness wore him down, made him lose confidence in his acting abilities. Despite past successes, he began doubting that he had ever had any talent. Well, perhaps there was a bit of gunpowder in his flask, but apparently just enough for a small spark. On such days, his side began aching. He imagined that some vile sickness had got to him, cancer or some other disease of the same mean spirit.

He was born in Voronezh; he studied and graduated from the prestigious State School for Theatrical Arts in Moscow. Then he found a job in his native city. Voronezh City Theatre was of good, sound quality and stable reputation. Once, when the Leningrad Drama Theatre was on tour in the city, the director saw him playing the part of Firs, Mrs. Ranevsky's old butler in Chekhov's *Cherry Orchard*. The director was quite impressed with his performance and invited him to join his company. Of all the parts Semyon played—and, for twenty-some years of his career, he accumulated quite a few of them—Firs was his special success. It comprised just a handful of lines, but he enjoyed this part so much! There were other lucky breaks as well, but concerning this particular part, a journalist once told him warmly: "You play Firs as if you were born inside of him."

In the play, when Mrs. Ranevsky moves out, she forgets about her old servant, leaving him behind in the empty rooms. *"They forgot about me!"* Semyon himself wondered how he managed to put so much into that final phrase just before the end of the play. He remembered how, when he had been preparing for the part, he struggled for a long time, looking for just the right tone for this phrase. How should he pronounce these few words so that they expressed Firs's whole sense of being, his whole life? After all, when moving, people may forget to take along some piece of furniture. But here it was a human being that was being disposed of. An old one, to be sure, but a human being all the same, not a chair, not a dresser . . . .

Semyon himself didn't know why this particular part came out so well. Maybe it was because he had been fond of Chekhov's works from his childhood, since that very day he had read the story "Kashtanka" for the first time. It's about a dog that lost her tippler of a master, a cabinet-maker by trade, in a crowd. Perhaps, because the story he read was published as a children's book, with illustrations, Semyon imagined the dog precisely the way she was drawn on its pages—a red-haired cross between a dachshund and a mongrel, affectionate and cheerful, her fluffy tail shaped like a question mark. It seemed the book itself gave off the aromas of fresh wood shavings, lacquer, and joiner glue that forever ensconced themselves in the dog's—and Semyon's—brain. Perhaps because his father worked as a carpenter and these smells were also smells of his own childhood, Semyon became firmly attached to "Kashtanka" with his whole soul.

He admired Chekhov not only as a writer. Rereading his biography, time and again he was impressed by the fact that the son of a shopkeeper and the grandson of a released serf found the spiritual strength to overcome the crude milieu of his upbringing. In Chekhov's childhood, his father beat the future writer for even a small blunder. Nevertheless, Chekhov took care of his parents in their old age. Semyon thought about Chekhov so frequently that he once caught himself thinking: if the writer would appear before him, he wouldn't be too surprised . . . .

❄ ❄ ❄

The decision to leave had been made, but this didn't relieve Semyon's anxiety. He still felt uneasy.

"Well, Syoma, don't get so bogged down!" Essy muttered. She moved around the room, trying to occupy herself with something. She rearranged shoes she had taken off at the entrance door when coming from the street. Drew the window curtains more fully closed. Turned the picture of her late father on the dresser so that it could catch the light of the desk lamp.

She, too, was anxious. It was one thing to blab about emigration at the kitchen table with your girlfriends, but quite another . . . . After all, there was no way back. You are stripped of Soviet citizenship, and you become a refugee, at the mercy of fate. You might as well be dead, since only the dead leave without ever being able to return.

"After all, everything has been heading this way, and for a long time," Essy continued, trying to calm him down and herself at the same time. "Aren't you tired of this life? There's more carbon monoxide than oxygen in the air here. Did you really intend to live like this forever?"

He shrugged. Why keep talking about it now, when the decision had been made already? Listening to his wife's grumbling, however, Semyon appreciated her tact. Going over again and again their reasons to emigrate, she spared his male pride. She didn't mention that, besides the pervasive shortage of oxygen, there was always a chronic shortage of money in their household. The fact was that he, a man, couldn't support his wife on his beggarly actor's salary. Together with Essy's income as a teacher of literature, they barely made ends meet. Thank God they didn't have any children—how could they afford even one child? And there was no use of even thinking about it now. Essy was past thirty-five. Struggling to survive, among other cares, they hadn't noticed that their youth had passed them by.

Well, of course he should have found a more lucrative occupation. But what was there for him to do if he was never drawn to anything besides acting? From childhood, from that very first school field trip to the Theatre of the Young Audience, he had fallen in love with the stage.

He adored theatre to the point of madness. He loved even the smell of paste and the dried-up stage-set paints, which gave off an indecent odor of sweaty feet. From the first moment of a new play reading around the table, he couldn't wait for the director's staging. He frequently stayed behind in the theatre after everybody else headed home so that, text in hand, he could circle the stage, trying out where would be the best spot for his character to position himself when saying his lines. When he moved around, even the wooden floor's creaking under him gave him sweet shivers. Theatre! What a remarkable invention! What would his life be if not for acting? He even had a secret childish fear: what if everyone discovered what extraordinary joy acting was? They would abandon their boring trades—bookkeepers, drivers, or typists—and rush into the acting profession.

But now it was the early seventies. The Soviet economy had taken a nosedive, and Kremlin leaders were forced to seek Western favors in trading. The Cold War was temporarily mitigated by a policy that loosened tensions somewhat—in particular, the Soviet government yielded to political pressure from the West regarding its emigration policies. People began leaving quietly, one by one and two by two. Some went to Israel, some to America, some to Canada, and some to God knows where—to Australia, to New Zealand, to South Africa.

The preparations for leaving were long and painful. Semyon dragged out every chore, dawdled at every errand, no matter how small it was. Essy endured. She knew that he was trying to delay the inevitable.

The packing up shouldn't have taken a long time: they hadn't amassed many belongings. But there were quite a few books. Though they were read and re-read a long time ago, it turned out that they had become part of his and Essy's being; it was immensely hard to tear themselves away from them. After much struggle, Semyon decided to take along just an armful of books, only those he couldn't bring himself to leave behind. Among them was a three-volume set of Chekhov's selected works, in a blue dust jacket, and the "Kashtanka" booklet, which he had been emotionally attached to from his childhood and couldn't part with now no matter what.

Semyon spent the night before departure restlessly. In the intervals of dozing between hours of sleepless vigil, time suddenly began to crawl away under his hands as if it were a roll of old and dried-up wallpaper coming off in layers. Before his eyes, as if on a film rewinding, his whole life flashed by. The streets of Voronezh. The student years in Moscow, filled with vague but bright dreams of fame. Touring with his troupe around the country. The rounds of applause, rising and abating, as if they were huge ocean waves . . . .

And then a bell rang out—not the melodious sound of a curtain call, which usually sent a chill of excitement up his spine, but the harsh clatter of the alarm clock. Semyon jumped to his feet. It was time to go to the airport.

Their friends already awaited them. His father had come over from Voronezh. No matter how many times Semyon had tried to persuade him to leave with him, nothing came of it. "You go," his father replied. "It's normal for a human being to search for a better life. Don't worry about me. I get a solid, military pension."

Since the time of their last meeting, his father had aged terribly. His hair had turned entirely gray, and he leaned on a stick. Semyon embraced him, but in his heart he couldn't fully accept that most likely he was seeing him for the last time.

＊ ＊ ＊

They decided to settle in Brighton Beach, at the southern tip of Brooklyn. Over the years, a substantial enclave of Russian immigrants had come into being in that little town. When you start a new life it's easier to live among your own people. Some helped with advice; others gave them their old furniture. Essy got down to business vigorously. In *The New Russian Word*, an émigré paper, she spotted an ad about computer programming classes. She attended them for a few months and, to her own surprise—after all, she was a philologist, not a mathematician—she graduated with distinction, one of the best in her group. She quickly found a programmer's job. Luckily, at that time, for reasons unbeknownst to her, companies preferred to employ programmers who came from Russia, China, and India, who all had a sound education and were willing to work harder and longer for lower wages than Americans were.

Semyon also tried to master this new trade but eventually he gave it up. He couldn't stand it. Dry lines of computer code and purely brainy work that didn't demand imagination made him sick to his stomach.

In the afternoons, when staying home became unbearable, Semyon wandered around Brighton Beach. The neighborhood stunned him with its provincial appearance, unexpected in a country that was the embodiment of modernity. Freeways. . . . Skyscrapers . . . . Flights to the Moon . . . . And suddenly—unsightly two-story little houses, as might be found in some out-of-the-way Russian town like Elets or Serpukhov. Except that instead of rural silence, crashing was heard all around: subway trains rushed above ground here. Crowded little shops packed with groceries and household trifles nestled next to each other. There were newsstands on some street corners that sold pitiful little immigrant newspapers. All of these things reeked of terrible provincialism. And people's faces also seemed provincial, boring, in a state of stupor.

It was too depressing, and Semyon tried to convince himself that his eyes could deceive him. Probably, he saw others that way because he himself was frozen inside. He had noticed it a long time ago: when it happened he drank too much, the whole world seemed tipsy. And this place actually might not be dull at all. People were lively, noisy, and bustling about as if they poured out onto the streets from Sholom Aleichem's and Babel's stories. Once, as he wandered along Brighton Beach Boulevard, he spotted a page from a school notebook attached to an iron column supporting the subway rails; on it was written with a felt-tip pen: "Neighbors! Beware! Dentist Shapiro is a scalper!"

Within a few months, he found a few people in his neighborhood with whom he felt comfortable. Okunevsky, an artist, lamented that there was no demand in America for his paintings of the cozy nooks of the Black Sea resort towns Gurzuf and Anapa. Realism had long gone out of fashion. His work wasn't even considered art here. Gallery owners refused to take it on.

There was also Grandmaster Mikhail Lvovich. At his advanced age, he didn't take part in chess tournaments anymore, but thanks to his former fame he had found a few pupils, and this earned him some extra income to add to his modest Social Security.

But all the same, these men had nothing to do with the theatre. The conversations on general topics died out quickly. Okunevsky took to mastering abstract painting, but, though Semyon understood it intellectually, his heart didn't react to it and it was difficult for him to force out compliments. And the idea of playing chess with a grandmaster didn't even enter Semyon's brain. He would only shame himself.

The only comfort in Brighton Beach was the ocean. Semyon would take the boardwalk that stretched along the coast, wander on it for hours, and gradually his melancholy would dissipate. Next to the ocean's heaving giant waves, everything that burdened his soul seemed transient and unimportant. Peering into the ocean's distance, taking the fresh and invigorating air into his lungs, as much of it as possible, made him feel better.

The ocean reminded him of summer tours in the southern cities—in Kherson, in Odessa, in Yalta. There, he had warmed himself up after a long winter, bathed in the sea, and breathed in the spicy southern air, which seemed especially fragrant after Leningrad's odor of smog mixed with marsh-rot. He ate fresh tomatoes, cherries, and plums; in Leningrad, on his and Essy's paltry wages, they couldn't even get near them. During those tours, to fatten up actors, the theatre manager formed traveling performing brigades to work health resorts. Afterwards, as was the custom, the hosts set the table, fed the actors, served drinks, and pleased them in any way they could. They seated next to them influential people from among the vacationers—Party brass and retired high-ranking military men with their plump wives.

Though their standard compliments made Semyon cringe, he admitted secretly to himself that he was pleased to hear them. No matter what you say, any talent needs praise as mushrooms need showers. At the same time, he didn't take those compliments too much to heart. The moment you feel yourself riding high once and for all, your art comes to an end. He already took for granted that—despite years of experience—each new part was no easier than the previous one. "In art, the road always leads upwards," he reminded himself in Hans Christian Andersen's words, "up the red-hot ladder, but to heaven."

He loved going on tour because riding on trains and staying in hotels tore him away from his ordinary life and renewed his sensibilities. Traveling brought him together with a variety of people. He absorbed into himself everyone he encountered: a traveling companion, a train conductor, a porter, a waiter. He noticed how they talked, gestured, walked. You never knew what might some day come in handy on the stage.

In Yalta, he went more than once to a small Chekhov museum, in the house where his beloved writer used to live. There, in the silence of a small apartment where the writer, infected with tuberculosis, had spent the last years of his life, Semyon approached with awe Chekhov's personal belongings, lovingly laid out on little tables, under glass. He examined for a long time the dark suit with gray stripes, the pince-nez on a black braided cord, the narrow varnished shoes and bamboo walking stick.

Wandering along the Atlantic Ocean beach, Semyon reminded himself again and again that it was no use of thinking about all that now. All those things belonged to his past life, to which there was no return.

But he couldn't help it: he missed the theatre and his colleagues badly. When he moved along the boardwalk, time and again, he would think he spotted a familiar face in the crowd. Now that of the assistant director Aleksey Petrovich. Now that of the tragedian Stalsky. Now that of the comedian Pletnev. His heart pounding, he rushed towards them only to realize that, alas, he was mistaken. Yes, he said to himself, he may not have liked every one of them and, perhaps, not every one of them liked him, but they all lived similar lives and shared one passion.

From time to time, to calm himself down, he forced himself to think of everything bad about his actor's life. Of intrigues. Of gossips. Of behind-the-scene scheming. Of inept actors, relatives of some highly-placed government officials or Party bosses, who infiltrated his theatre on patronage, after a phone call.

He also recalled film shootings. He was invited as a character actor, sometimes, for an episode or two. He took the offer without much desire. He found living outside of his home, without Essy, lacking comfort. On film sets, they cared little about minor actors' living arrangements. A couple of times he even caught a serious chest cold. And he didn't like the work either: it involved very little art but more than enough humiliation. There, he often felt himself to be little more than a puppet. Now turn this way so the light will fall better on your face, now the other way. But what could be done? After all, he had a wife. And he always needed the money: film work paid very well.

But none of his efforts to dull his yearning for days past helped for long.

A few times, he and Essy took hour-long rides on the subway into Manhattan. Life there differed so sharply from Brighton that it seemed as if they played tourists visiting another English-speaking, country. They went to the Metropolitan Museum, to the

Guggenheim, to the Museum of Modern Art. There, it took them a while to come to their senses when they looked at a dog turd made of pig-iron and tried to see how this was an inquiry into a new means of artistic expression. They wandered around Times Square and its adjoining streets. They examined Broadway posters. They were surprised to find that musicals enjoyed such success in America. Not Shakespeare, not Tennessee Williams, not Bernard Shaw, but little operettas? Back in the Soviet Union, only the inhabitants of the merry city of Odessa were mad about such things. But was it proper for New York, the capital of the world?

Then they discovered a Broadway theatre staging Arthur Miller's *A View from the Bridge*. Semyon felt like seeing for himself what an American actor made of a part that, a few years ago, he himself had played back at his Leningrad theatre. His lack of English didn't bother him. He remembered the part, and he was convinced that a good actor can express suffering or joy even without words. Essy was about to buy tickets for that night's performance but Semyon looked up the prices and was terrified. For both of them, the evening out would run up to a hundred dollars. Was it true what the Soviet papers wrote—that only well-to-do people could afford theatre in America? Certainly, Essy wouldn't refuse him, but he was embarrassed. He already lived at his wife's expense as it was.

After that day, he began looking for work vigorously. Anything had to be better than sitting at home! After all, he was a healthy man, not a hanger-on. Without speaking the language, certainly, it wasn't easy, but, after persistent searches, he found a job as a night watchman in a medical equipment shop. Everything for the handicapped: crutches, wheelchairs, and walkers. He went to the store late every evening and caught up on his sleep when he got back in the morning.

Whether because of his place of work or for some other reason, when he came home at daybreak and went to bed, the same single dream visited him. He was back in his theatre rehearsing a scene. He was lying on his back on a stretcher, and some roughnecks started dragging him somewhere, with enthusiasm.

"Hey!" he shouted in fear, opening his eyes. "Where are you taking me, devils?"

"What do you mean, where?" they snorted, puffing their smelly hand-rolled cigarettes. "Where else are we to take you, dear friend, if not to the morgue?"

"The morgue?" he cried out. "Have you gone mad? What are you talking about? I'm still alive!"

And the roughnecks guffawed: "We aren't there yet!"

And he woke up in cold sweat.

The dream made his heart pound. Semyon walked to the beach, loafed along the boardwalk, greedily catching the gusts of ocean wind in his nostrils. Then he returned home. Waiting for Essy to come from work, he sat at the table and smoked, thinking of how he was going live from now on.

One evening, he sat as usual in the semi-darkness and smoked. Feeling drowsy, he put his head on his arm bent at the elbow, fighting with himself not to doze off. Essy would soon come home from work. They would have dinner, and then he would go to guard his store. Suddenly he got the strange feeling that some-one was sitting in the chair next to him. He froze, listening intently. But he didn't hear anything except what seemed to be the other chair creaking slightly.

Without lifting his eyes, without seeing a black braided cord hanging down from the pale dry temple, without hearing the characteristic lung patient's intermittent cough, he somehow knew *who* his visitor was. Anton Pavlovich Chekhov himself, in person. At the same moment, he got a strong feeling that had sometimes visited him in the past—that time wasn't an abstraction but some kind of substance melting in front of his eyes. As in Dali's paint-ings, it became flabby; it sagged as if it were just about to drip onto their Brighton apartment parquet floor, which was, out of their old Leningrad habit, polished to a shine.

"*It cannot be because it can never be*"—the famous phrase com-posed by his guest in his youth, which Semyon liked to repeat whenever an opportunity presented itself, flashed in his head.

He was still deciding whether he had just imagined that face in the semi-darkness, when the man cleared his throat and uttered quietly, but clearly, "Well, dear host, shall we drink some tea? Or perhaps something stronger? You should treat your guests to something."

What the hell's happening to me? Semyon asked himself. *I should make an effort and pull myself together.* He stood up and without look-ing back walked to the bathroom, where he splashed some water onto his face. When he returned to the living room the man at the table apparently hadn't even thought of disappearing: he propped up his head on his palm and looked at Semyon with a good-natured smile.

Semyon went to the kitchen and took two cups and saucers out of the cupboard. Then he turned to the refrigerator. *Should I open a beer? Heineken, perhaps? What about beer mugs? There should be some in the freezer. Where the hell is Essy?* He knew that this wasn't fair. If she ever came home late from work it was because she had stopped by a supermarket on her way home to buy something for dinner.

Extraordinary vigor seized him, the kind that he remembered getting during dress rehearsals, when he knew that the part was turning out well. From nowhere, some energy would suddenly fill his whole body. He picked up the cups, the saucers, and the teaspoons from the shelf. He carried the dishes to the table and felt joy. *Ah, wonderful! What's going on with me just means that I'm still capable of getting agitated. For the first time in all my American life, I'm excited! That means I'm alive again. That counts for something.*

As he reached the table, the electric teapot clicked, signaling that water had boiled. Semyon didn't dare to look at the visitor's face again, only at the thin hands sticking out from the cuffs of his dark old-fashioned jacket with gray stripes. Ah, come what may!

"Hello, Anton Pavlovich," Semyon said without lifting his head.

And he heard the reply: "Hello, Samuil Moiseevich."

Semyon winced. No one had called him by his true first name and patronymic since the Visa Department in Moscow took his passport away and gave him a pinkish piece of paper in exchange—his exit visa. He was about to correct his guest, to tell him what he told everyone back home and still was telling everyone here, in Brighton—that his name is Semyon Mikhailovich. But the sound of his guest's voice, quiet and pleasant, struck Semyon dumb.

Meanwhile, the man at the table used the pause to make a soft remark: "Why are you ashamed of your own name? Samuel is the name of a biblical prophet. And your patronymic comes from the name that anyone would be proud to bear: the name of Moses, the leader and lawmaker of a great people."

Semyon began mechanically pouring the tea into the cups, when suddenly he smiled. Why hadn't he thought of it right away? It's all too simple—his friends were putting him on. It was either Okunevsky or Mikhail Lvovich. Both had a sense of humor. They'd decided to play a trick on him, and persuaded some immigrant, perhaps another former actor like himself, to make himself up to look like Chekhov. As to the ancient walking stick and the pince-nez on a braided cord, you can find anything in American antique shops.

Out of the corner of his eye, he glanced at his visitor again. The spitting image of Chekhov! A masterful makeup job. *I shall behave myself cautiously so as not to give the jokers too much satisfaction.*

He forced himself to sit down next to the visitor and began drinking tea, feverishly thinking of how to bring the pranksters out into the open. He recalled that, on the blue dust jacket of the three-volume set of Chekhov's works he had brought with him, there was the facsimile of the writer's signature. *I'll ask for his autograph, and then, after all this is over, if Okunevsky begins laughing, I'll show that I knew all along that they were playing a trick on me. I will verify the guest's handwriting against the signature. Let them try to get out of it then.*

It seemed that the guest read his thoughts: he turned towards the bookshelf and, as if he had known beforehand exactly where it was located, pulled out the thin volume of *Kashtanka*. He hummed with satisfaction and, with a ballpoint pen that appeared out of nowhere, inscribed on the flyleaf: "To Samuil Moiseevich Spielman, for memory's sake on the occasion of our meeting in Brighton Beach." And he signed it.

At first, Semyon rejoiced now that he had his proof. But he also wished that the visitor would just up and disappear as suddenly as he had appeared. Then everything in his life, though not too happy, but which he had already started getting used to, would fall into place.

But long minutes went by, and the visitor clearly had no intention of vanishing. *I should stall. Essy will come home, and then everything will clear up.*

But he found waiting unbearable. He needed to do something and do it right away.

Suddenly it dawned on him. Why hadn't he thought of it at once?

"Well," he said to his guest as calmly as he could. "Why do we sit in a stuffy room, Anton Pavlovich? Why don't we take a walk? I'll show you Brighton."

"I adore walks," the visitor said without the slightest confusion. He squinted for a moment, took off his pince-nez, wiped the lenses clean with a little flannel cloth, and put it in his pocket. Then he picked up his walking stick. "I'm ready."

Semyon let him pass to the door and followed, his legs weak.

As soon as they'd left the apartment, they ran into a young black boy named Charlie, a hired hand at Boris's grocery store at the corner of Brighton and Coney Island Boulevards.

"Hi, Charlie," Semyon said. "Let me introduce you. Here's Anton Pavlovich Chekhov."

"Hi, Tony," Charlie said, waving his hand and flashing a smile.

Well, this one's so-so as a witness, Semyon thought, *I should find one of our Russian people.*

He led his guest to the boardwalk, which, at this hour, was usually filling up with strolling couples. No one paid any attention to them. Semyon was again seized with anxiety. *Am I seeing things? But the black boy greeted the visitor, didn't he?*

Right then, among the passersby, the familiar figure of an old man appeared. It was a Russian poet nicknamed "The Falcon." He got his nickname because of the tempestuous look of his piercing eyes from under his shaggy eyebrows, as well as his gait—he moved sideways, dragging his leg slightly, stooping under the weight of a heavy bag on his shoulder packed with volumes of verses of his own composition. He indeed resembled a wounded bird incapable of soaring.

In his native land, the old man had been a member of the privileged Union of Soviet Writers. In Moscow, in a building near the Airport subway station that housed writers exclusively, he occupied a big comfortable apartment. The most prestigious publishing houses put his books out. By Soviet standards, he was rich. He drove a Muscovite car and married in succession a number of beautiful young women. Apparently, his success went to his head. Once discontent with the authorities became fashionable among his fellow writers, he began writing daring little poems seeking popularity among them. These poems began to circulate in the underground, and he soon got in trouble. He was expelled from the Writers' Union. When he was evicted from the prestigious building in which he lived, the beautiful young women lost interest in him altogether. Eventually, he had no choice but to leave the country, and finally wound up in Brighton Beach. Here he wandered from restaurant to restaurant, where he would sneak up on diners and, without giving them an opportunity to come to their senses, throw down on the table in front of them a booklet printed at his own expense, proclaiming in a hoarse dramatic voice:

"My last collection! Ten years of backbreaking labor! The full price is ten dollars. A dollar per a year of a writer's toil. You must agree that it isn't much. But for you—only eight dollars and not a cent more!"

As the old man neared them, Semyon waved at him and said in a nervous voice:

"Grigory Osipovich, look who's visiting us. Anton Pavlovich!"

His shaggy eyebrows moving, Falcon froze for a moment, scrutinized the one who called to him and then his companion. Then he tore the bag off his shoulder, snatched out a lean brochure and rushed to Semyon's guest: "My dear, do an honor to a fellow writer! Please accept this as a gift. At least you will read my work. Just look at them," he threw his hand up in a broad gesture that encompassed the crowd of passersby. "Does poetry interest them? Back in Russia, the KGB chased after me! They read every comma I wrote. They dragged me to interrogations. And, mind you, there I was just an apprentice. Here I have produced my best work. But these people don't give a damn about it! They refuse to read it! Do you want to know what they find worthy of hot discussion? I'll tell you what! It is the sacramental question: 'Which cabbage in the supermarket International Food is better, sauerkraut with olive oil or pickled with cowberries?' Ah! Was it worth it for me to endure persecutions and suffer for these people?"

Semyon couldn't wait to get away from him. He tried to shield the visitor, who suddenly had a fit of coughing. Semyon's temples ached. The lanterns along the wooden flooring seemed to take off from the posts and begin sailing in the evening air. *I'm walking along the boardwalk with Chekhov. It's a joke. All this is just one silly joke.*

To suppress the anxiety that had suddenly captured him, Semyon said hesitantly: "Anton Pavlovich, listen! Perhaps it's worth a try. Since you're here already, why won't you see a doctor?"

What gibberish am I carrying on?—flashed in his brain, but he found it difficult to stop: "I know a former luminary of Soviet medicine. He used to be a corresponding member of the Soviet Academy of Science. Without an American license, he goes to waste here. Your—shall we say, ailment," for some reason, Semyon found it too coarse to say the word "tuberculosis," "is now easily treated in America."

The visitor burst out into a delightful laugh: "Thank you for caring, Samuil. But you know, my dear friend, death is always un-timely and out of place. When it paid a visit to me, I was just forty-four and far away from my native land. In Germany, of all places. Everyone's given only what's written for them in the Book of Life. And we don't have the power to change that, do we? Few artists have the luck of having enough time to do everything they aspire to do. One should thank his good fortune for what he has managed to accomplish. That's the way it is, my friend."

Lost in thought over what was said, Semyon didn't notice as they stopped at the International Food supermarket. There, the visitor took his pince-nez out of his pocket and examined with great curiosity the sausages hanging from the ceiling, the pickles in little barrels, the cake pyramids, and the round-shaped ladies crowding the counters. Their faces expressed the importance of their deliberations, as if they were choosing not some appetizers but dresses for a governor's ball.

Then he said, shaking his head: "I believe that, in one of my stories, I lamented over how sad it is to live in the world. Well, it turns out to be quite jolly, at least for some."

Semyon felt suddenly tired, almost on the verge of collapsing from exhaustion.

As if sensing it, the visitor began bidding goodbye. He need-ed, he said, to be alone for a while. Being himself a creative person, his host should understand it. He tipped his hat:

"Give your spouse my best regards, Samuil Moiseevich. What's her name, forgive me? Essy? That means Esther. Give your Esther my best regards, will you?"

With this, he whistled lightly, and, from somewhere in the depths of the store, a red-haired dog with a clever fox's muzzle and a fluffy tail jumped out. The visitor scratched it behind its ear. The dog wagged its tail in pleasure and, when the visitor turned to the ocean, it trotted at his feet, from time to time raising its head as if trying to glance at his face.

Semyon inhaled deeply. Instead of the usual Brighton

smell—a mixture of salty ocean air and burnt gasoline—the aroma
of wood spirit, resin, and glue filled the air. It made him feel he was
a child again, back in his native land, playing on the floor of his
father's shop. His sadness began to release him. Yes, he was God
knows how far from Leningrad, from his native Voronezh. But this
didn't matter anymore. For the first time, peace and quiet settled
into his soul. And, perhaps, for the first time, he now understood
a line from Pushkin whose full meaning he had never grasped before: *Pechal' moia svetla*, "My sorrow is filled with light."

He needed to hurry home. Essy was probably already long
back from work and wondering where he was. He walked along
the embankment. From the loudspeaker on the roof of a café, a
simple song reached him. Before he quickened his step, he looked
back. Nearby, on the beach, at the very waterline, in the faltering
light of lanterns swaying in the wind, there stood a tall thin man
in pince-nez, wearing a straw hat with a black ribbon. He wore an
elegant coat of old-fashioned cut and held a walking stick in his
hand. He stirred the pebbles, apparently thinking of something. He
peered into the thickening haze of the ocean, squinted as he smiled,
muttered something to himself and coughed slightly. At his feet, a
red-haired dog danced about. Time and again, it lifted its muzzle to
look attentively at the waves, as if waiting for something to emerge
from them any minute now, something that would surprise it and
make it happy.

Nathan Opp, *Subway Stop View*, oil on canvas

Salt

The truth is that one of us
will be left alone, and soon.
Death does not care which one.
Someone will wear out, disappear,
someone stay behind to wait
with ashes and tiny bones,
body fluids, rumpled sheets,
rings of white residue
on the bedside table,
coins between cushions.
One of us will look back,
nameless as Lot's wife,
head torqued over the shoulder,
desperate for one last look
at the two of us,
not moving, holding on
to old photos, poems, ticket stubs.
How to prepare for it?
A word, a finger tracing an ear?
Hurry, before one of us
feels the stiffening of limbs
the tap on the shoulder,
pressure on wrist,
before a dry palm sweeps
across the eyelids,
and the anonymous one
is sculpted into a question mark,
who is? who was? —
words sprinkled
like grains on the tongue.

Psalm

Without a word, you did this for me:
gathered my whites, my darks,

spot-cleaned my green sweater, sorted
my underpants, underwire bras, nightgown,

separated out the gray-soled gym socks,
removing crumpled tissues from my black jeans,

turning them inside out, set aside my red blouse
with the pearl buttons for special attention.

All the while, I wrote poems upstairs
listening to the whoosh of hot water,

the tumbling of snaps and zippers,
heard you shake out the wrinkles,

your wedding band clinking on the folding table
as you straightened my shoulders, buttoned my fronts,

felt for dampness, tenderly pressing cottons and silks
with your dry hands, as the scent of cleanliness

released from the dryer drifted up the steps.
You let me be; my throat catches in gratitude —

my things laid out on our bed, folded square,
crotches tucked, cups nestled inside one another,

bleached soles, matched in pairs and rolled,
arms bent at the elbow hugging my spotless torso.

Without a word, all accounted for, shining.

World Without End

Leaving the children to niggle and spit
while she lingered at the handsome
neighbor's house, mother did what humans do
when battered or bored or simply afraid.
And father did what young men do
after their wheelless bomber skids down
on desert tarmac while the crewmen
cry out their mothers' names.

They did what the dead have always
done—shouldered bricks on steep
ramps, obeyed the boss, cleaned
the children's ears with painted
fingernails. Made do with hardened
bread and onions fried in chicken fat.
They gave precisely what they knew
to give and made me who I am.

They did what animals do—hunger on their
young's account. Mother dished up
nubbly cow's tongue and father
a Motorola TV and blue Rambler.
They locked the front door to keep love in
where it nuzzled, and shielded, spasmed
and flailed. And it was enough
so that I can do what humans do.

Theories of Evolution

History says

The heart was an undersea creature. While pre-
platypi raised their oiled bodies to shore fighting air,
the heart bobbed in the swamp, ventricle up. Such a
decisive tick that even alligators left it be. Sloppy,
pudding-black, thick as a fist before there were fists,
snail-like. During a storm it got washed to high land.
Spent, it squeezed into a glossed knot, then napped
between two ribs that lay cracked open by the sea.
Some things you think are carrion turn out not to be.
When it woke, the bone-cage had gathered other parts
from what drifted in, then sealed shut. Cells formed
around the heart, all eyes on its deck. Such pearlized
pressure—liquid quartz, liquid rose—heart's own
force driving the machine. Its telescoping echo.

Human says

My heart is named Henry, for alliteration, and often
          he wants out. *There, there, driving fist. There, there*
hot locomotive, horse that will not break. Your rearing
          shoves us forward. I'd spring the catch
and usher him to the nearest wading pool if it wasn't
          for logistics. At night, I knock at the ribbed vault
so he hears something other than his own hum.
          I pantomime splitting the ribs, letting him nose out.
How's that for compassion.

Organ says

Morse code   to human   frame:
          make us   a new artery
from felt   soak it in milk
          cut open   the lung
and insert.   Little plug
          thick   and bloodless.
Pull in   new substance.

Organ says (translation)

Moon comes like a full orange to the garden. We deserve to be afloat again.

The Disowning

My mother packs me butter-pears, bread, a woolen blanket,
and says *go to a temperate climate, wash often,*
sleep alone. Then she closes the door of her face
and leaves me. Outside is gray with fog. I have
cut my hair off at the root. Father stops splitting

wood, lays down the blade and begins the act
of forgetting. My sisters, blond twins,
stand rigid, small, hands thrust in their pockets.
Four brown boots toe in and hush. One hands me
a buck knife for skinning, the other unties

a ribbon from her hair. Maps do not exist here.
Beyond the town, forest. Beyond the forest,
swamp, more forest. Animals I do not know.
Gods I do not know. The same rotation
of sky, carrying nothing human.

Figurine

Because he wore that saucepan on his head
day and night,
even in the bath,

everybody thought he was a genius.

The girls,
their dresses domed like mushroom caps,

and the boys, identical
except for the colors of their clothes—the same
hard smiles, same three freckles on each cheek,
same bald plastic heads.

Only Pan Head wore a hat.

We arrange them on the grass,
take turns picking. Houses first,
then furniture, the people last—and Jenny,

with her scalloped collar and her little helmet
of brown hair,
always mine. I like to have her
venture to the asphalt with the heat
of the day still in it, ants and earwigs
climbing from the cracks. The blossoms dropping
from the silk floss tree
she grinds to dust
beneath the barrel of her body.

Jenny could have any boy,
but Pan Head is the one she asks
to walk with her
beyond the billowing petunias, clods of dirt
as big as boulders.
What must she be thinking? She must want

to make him take it off.
She wants to pry the plastic
from his head, see the bald skin
wrinkled like my brother's thumb,
always red and crooked
from so much sucking.

Sand Dollars

You line the salt-warped railing of the porch,
arranged by size.
The largest of you, scum-stained green
and dull, like everything the ocean makes
old with persistent touch, repel
me, but you
smallest disks, the print of your five
petals faint,
child nipples, accidental
drops of batter on the griddle,
you glint brighter
than the gutters of the house, or the bone —
bare apple branches, or my own
white, restless hands — do you remember
the ocean bottom dark, your life before
we met, when you would creep
on fine, tubed feet
and, furred in purple
spines, swallow sand and pocket it
to weight yourselves
against the tide?

Greenbottle the Elder

When the second deluge came
I had no prophet's beard to cringe behind.
I stayed alive—afloat—through breath
and a certain dove-feathered angel named *fear*.

Where bodies washed up, there was I:
relieved beyond belief to have
so many morsels: a feast upon the sand.
And then there was the winter

I ate cows whole and grew twenty feet—
the villagers tried to come and adore,
which soothed and sufficed
until the last bull's bones were clean:

ashes under bare beams, children's teeth
scattered like corn in barn dirt—
all that was left. Now, the kernel
I've shrunk to hunkers below the sun

thirsting for whatever sign that star wants
to bestow: a breath of wind rending trees,
a clutch of ribs moored in the flora,
a certain crow-feathered angel named *hope*.

Starlit Abattoir

Which direction, Sir Greenbottle, are the vernal storms pulsing tonight—east, west, or out of the south? These acres wait for you to hit upon a new guise, a fresh sin for you to immerse yourself in—slowly, a thought at a time, the manner in which a front swings willy-nilly with its blue or red teeth across our states. From stasis, from the bone-stench and blood rainbow of my desk, the window is your lone portal unto weather, your elevator (up or down, depending) to the sacred. My work is in spinal barometers, mechanisms of gland torn from throat or limb to make more than one word work as the carnage of my method fan-tails behind me, a pattern of exotic gore and lunar cartilage. Up the road your mutt is yowling again, holding forth about claims on lakes and hills, basements and attics. My weapon grows dull but makes the labor more meaningful. Stockades of cloud assemble on either horizon but for now the stars look in on the cuts I've arranged, the few stays that have proven themselves against you, my muttered hymns that yet resound—the stars are just one gear to an infinite clockworks and tonight they offer some light.

Emily Dickinson Stays Home When Ralph Waldo Emerson Visits Her Brother's House

Let there be no argument
from the grass between
my brother's house and mine.
No need to touch flesh —

like the Word, he must glow.
Hadn't we met in that place
where Dream is born —

I remember — Soul sparks
erupted — I felt
my own ignite —
in my ear — *the Mountains straight reply.*

Origins

Your newborn head,
heavy with prior life
that will flush away
like the afterbirth,
ignites the crook of my arm.
You are hunger, one-half
of the moon's shine. Your name is
lemon on the tongue—
a godparent's gossip.

*

You command me
to read another one.
Seuss or Puss in Boots,
it is not the story
that matters.
You sink in my lap,
a Buddha in footed pajamas.
Tonight I am
your servant, your family.

*

You join your sisters,
single file, on the treadmill—
sugarcane stalks, each
humming different tunes
that dovetail. You
swing your arms and laugh
as you march nowhere
but gain everywhere.
Silly. Blessed.

Safety Net

In the community of oil-field roughnecks, my dad
was hands-down champ. With a fourth-grade education
and a fistful of colorful cusses, he wove elaborate

patterns of speech that caught him the day the winch-line
chewed two fingers off his left hand, and the morning he found
Clyde floating in the slush-pit with his mouth full of tar, and

when fire traveled up the derrick faster than Dell
could ladder down, and during the Great Depression's iron
crush, and the night my mother told him the cancer was back.

Solitudes of a Manufacturer's Rep

> You should try to think
> seriously for a while
> every day.
> —*Miss Byars,*
> *eleventh-grade civics*

His name is Alfred.
Track him from town to town
in the prime of his ego,

how he leans against the railing of an overlook,
eases an August afternoon at the countyline bar,

overtaken by restless ironies,
the intertwining of things,
mismeetings, unfinished conversations,
the turning years.

You understand.

It is an idiomatic face,
not unappealing,
the leaves of the sumac gone red,
not unintelligent,
the fog dead white along the river road,

his cheeks ruddy where the shadow falls,
grasshoppers whirring,
deer grazing at the edge of the woods,
and falls again,
jonquils growing wild around a crumbling chimney.

You understand.

He perceives in himself a superfluous man.

A common, a negligible man
whose pride of private worth,
his rights and dignities,
his tender viscera,

do not transpire into public worth.

Track him from town to town
in the prime of his ego,
gray geese calling,
honeysuckle climbing a rain spout,
the snow plows out at dawn.

His name is Alfred.

LEE ROSSI

The Apartment

What good is it to have so many ideas
but understand almost nothing
about your life,

the way a lighthouse on steroids
will pump its million-candlepower clarity
into a fog's endless gnashing?

I sat at a wobbly kitchen table, talking with
my best friend's beautiful, unstable girlfriend
while in the next room he made love to her roommate.

I suppose we were being polite in the observant,
optimistic way of young people who sense
that finally they have something dreadful

to talk about, something that even their parents
would admit marks them
as people who've begun to live.

"No guts, no glory," we used to say,
like truck drivers knocking back coffee in some bleary diner
after a night of 90-mile-an-hour benzedrine.

I took another sip and tried to imagine
what Sartre, that inspired womanizer,
would say to this uncomprehending girl,

her eyes focused on the No-Pest Strip
gathering tenants in the air above us
and not on the door between the kitchen

and the only other room in the place.
How could we take the darkness we'd been given
and make our own vivid and exacting darkness,

so deep, so profound not even Sartre
could find his way home before the fog of desire,
or whatever it was, had lifted

and the sun shot its flashlight
into our guilty faces
like a cop, leering and tired?

Nathan Opp, *Oblique*, oil on canvas

Reading Hayden's Frederick Douglass to the Dealers

Like attaching safety pins on baby diapers
I tie a Windsor knot over the alleged drug dealer's shoulder.
The brightly colored Salvation Army ties
I bought in bulk before my lecture
flutter like big box kites at Cesar Chavez Park
around their muscled necks.

Twelve recently arrested alleged street dealers, eighteen to twenty-one,
sit around the conference table at Probation Hall,
executives in their orange molded plastic chairs.
I try to mentor them by measuring their necks
and arms; I teach them how to iron shirts.

My auntie showed me how says one.
She flicks the water from a bowl like that he demonstrates.
I use one of them clip-ons says another boldly.
The lady probation officer interrupts
Uh-huh, you still need to learn how to tie a tie.
When I recite the Hayden poem they won't look up.

Halloween

Evening and the fever of sunset
pinks the white patches on the Holsteins.
In her cabin, the hot throat of the pellet stove
swallows switchgrass and dust.

All afternoon at the hospital, she'd slit open
care packages from the patients' families
with a letter opener, snapped pumpkin-colored ribbon,
defoiled milk chocolate witches with latex gloves.
All clean as a barber's blade.

She steps into the yard with the dog,
feels the first snow in the hills just beyond reach
like a coyote pacing the pasture fence.
At the side of the road, turkey vultures

raindance in slated moonlight
around the remains of a fawn and tug at its thigh
with surgical tenderness, their shrunken heads
bobbing like paper lanterns on a summer zephyr.

Flirting with Normal, Flirting with Crazy

Elissa and I were in the same grade only senior year. She didn't graduate with her own class, a year ahead of mine, because she'd missed so much school, hospitalized in Pineville and too busy being crazy to focus on chemistry or anything else.

The summer before that school year started, the state decided to blacktop the country road running in front of my house. Parades of dump trucks, overflowing with gravel and dirt, streamed past the front porch where I sat and watched. The source of all that dirt and gravel was a mystery, but the supply was endless. Trucks traveled north with full loads, then returned empty.

Charlotte, who changed her name to Charley sophomore year because it sounded like a person ready for fun, called when the trucks were dumping their loads miles from my house. "You'll never guess," she said.

"Probably not." I was never one for smart retorts. I blamed my parents, who gave me a name, Belinda, which didn't lend itself to clever transformation and forecast a plain life, not a brilliant one.

"Guess who'll be in our class in September."

"Elissa Barberot," I said. My mother had heard the news that morning during a visit to the corner store where our as yet unpaved road met the highway. I'd already been admonished to be friendly whenever I saw Elissa. My mother craved friendly children and I was the disappointment of her life.

"You know." Charley's voice went from breathy excitement, her groundbreaking voice, to the "poor me" tone I found so irritating. When she wasn't first with news, she drew consolation from being ahead of me. This time, there wasn't even that. "You should've called. I called you right away."

"Mama's been on the phone until this minute," I lied.

"Well all right then." She was only partly mollified, as if I should've snatched the phone from my mother in the middle of the conversation I'd just invented.

Since Charlotte became Charley, she was more demanding in what she expected of our friendship. I was used to being the foil for her looks and personality. She was small-boned and had hair that hung in thick, straight strands. I was too tall and while my dark, almost black, hair was occasionally an asset, it frizzed at the first hint of rain. Charley got jokes right away, gauged what was required of her in most situations and reacted without hesitation. In contrast, I was often caught off balance, my responses a fraction off the beat. Standing next to me, Charlotte looked better than when she stood alone. But now that she'd become Charley, more was required of me and I wasn't sure I was up to it all. "Anyway," she said, "can you believe it? I didn't think they'd let her out so soon."

"Why not? She's been gone months." Last year, just before Thanksgiving, the news had spread across school, person to person, class to class, until the halls blazed with the latest misadventures of our own crazy girl.

"But this time, she cut her wrist. In the bathtub." Charley was breathy again, as titillated as if the news were brand-new.

"Her wrist," I repeated. Had Elissa dropped the razor in the tub or tossed it over the side? I blinked away the picture of blood and water and Elissa in the middle of it all.

"You wouldn't think they'd let someone back in school after she did something like that."

"It's the law," I said. "They don't have a choice."

"Really?" The question wasn't a challenge. Charley didn't mind being the one not knowing anything about laws.

"If she wants to come back, the school has to let her," I said. Outside, a truck rumbled past, blew its horn at my ten-year-old brother, Eugene, who'd pumped his arm furiously to win the blast.

"Do you think anyone will let her sit at their table?" Charley asked. "There's no law about that."

Cafeteria tables were claimed by various cliques, an arrangement making our lives simpler because you always knew where you belonged, even if it was at the three-girl table of leftovers. "Maybe Vicky's table." I named one of those three. Where else would Elissa fit?

"Right. Vicky's table. I should've thought of that." She sounded relieved. Had she been afraid of Elissa choosing our table, forcing us to study the faint scar on her wrist, her left because she was right-handed like most of us?

Back on the front porch, I watched trucks—full, then empty, then full again—roll past. Unlike Eugene, I didn't draw attention to myself, but sometimes, even unsolicited, a driver spotted me and blew his horn. When that happened this late July day, I waved.

Acting as expected is usually the smart way to go. I learned that a long time ago.

❋   ❋   ❋

Like every other high school girl, I selected my outfit for the first day with special care. We girls scrutinized each other daily, but most especially on that first day. If you couldn't dress acceptably for the first day, how could you possibly manage the rest of the year? Expect to be elected to homecoming court or chosen sweetheart of some club for the Spring Flowers Festival?

Last year, Charley was an alternate sweetheart for the Future Teachers of America in the April festival. That wasn't much of a club and certainly didn't represent her ultimate ambition, but it was a start. After that? We both understood anything was possible. She'd worn a lavender gown to compliment her auburn hair. Along with the other alternates, none of them eligible to be chosen queen, she paraded across the gym floor and stopped before the judges' table to curtsey. Each of those alternates hoped for more next time, saw this as their beginning just as Charley did.

Charley had practiced that curtsey for hours in front of her bedroom mirror as I watched. We were quite a pair—Charley in her elegant dress, me in jean cut-offs, two opposites reflected in the same mirror. "Am I doing it right? Should I drop lower to the floor?" How was I supposed to know?

Some time during all the practicing in her bedroom, I'd accepted that I had no chance of ever being selected to promenade across the gym floor. But during my long summer, reality was displaced by hope when the impossible again felt within reach. I hadn't gained an inch during the summer and thought I might've finally stopped growing. Then the first day of school arrived and Charley wore dark lipstick while mine remained the pale pink of last spring. At that moment, I knew senior year was doomed to the same pattern marked by my other years.

Charley ran up as soon as she spotted me crossing the courtyard. "Did you see her?"

"Who?" I glanced at other students, already divided into various allegiances.

"Elissa. Did you see Elissa yet?" She passed her tongue across her lips, a habit she nursed after reading, in one of her fashion magazines, about the sensuality of moistened lips.

"I only just got here." I covered my bottom lip with my left thumb. At least my skirt was of the proper style. In all those summer conversations, why hadn't she told me my lipstick shade was passé? How could I satisfy expectations, if I didn't know what they were?

"She looks like a nun practically." She hooked my elbow with one hand and directed me forward. "See her? On the steps?"

Though I couldn't distinguish features from this distance, there was no mistaking the figure sitting on the edge of the wide cement column framing the steps leading into the brick building. Our own crazy girl. She wore a nondescript beige jumper and yellow blouse. Her legs dangled over the edge, her back as straight and stiff as the column. Did Pineville provide posture lessons as well as shock treatments?

"She hasn't spoken to anyone." Charley squeezed my elbow. "Do you think the treatments did something to her voice? Changed it so she sounds like a boy? Or squeals like a baby? Or maybe . . ." Here she squeezed me twice. "Maybe she can't talk above a whisper, her voice burned out of her."

I tried to appear enthusiastic about those possibilities, enthusiasm being a hallmark of anyone with a chance for the homecoming court. But my false face didn't fool Charley who'd known me too many years.

"Just a thought," she said. She dropped my arm to let me find my own way. "She isn't wearing makeup, not even lipstick. You have to agree with me there," she said as if I were in the habit of disagreeing with someone who hovered on the edge of becoming one of the girls who glowed in high school. If that happened, I'd absorb some of her reflected glory, better than no glory at all. "She looks like a ghost. Really she does."

I nodded, though Elissa was too far away for me to make this observation on my own. "She's alone," I said. Even from this distance, I could see that for myself.

"Well of course." She made the isolation seem so inevitable as to be unworthy of comment.

The first bell of the first day rang and students drifted in groups of three, four, five towards the flagpole planted in the middle of a circle of grass, itself surrounded by a circular sidewalk with other walks radiating from its outer rim and leading to classroom buildings, the cafeteria, or the gym. All walks eventually led to that flagpole on the front grounds of the school and so it was natural to begin the year there, the place where all lines converged.

The sun shone as it had for every one of my first days of school, bright promises of days to come. We seniors arranged ourselves in the arc of circle facing the main school building. Juniors and sophomores gathered on either side of us. Freshmen were relegated to the least desirable position, their backs to the school as befit their lowly station in life. So it had always been and so it would always be.

When the principal, Mr. Gutierrez, said his first words, the scuffling and talking and laughing stopped. Only on this morning, of all mornings, did he command our full attention. Every year, for those first few moments, we hoped for a revelation of what we could be, a vision of our futures. It was first day and we yearned for new possibilities. Knowing that, you'd think he would've planned special words of inspiration and welcome. But every year, Mr. Gutierrez was underwhelming, impervious to or unaware of the desires thrumming in each of us. Instead, his comments were identical to the ones we'd heard all last year and the years before. Work hard. Obey rules. Listen to teachers. Stay out of trouble. Behind me, two girls whispered, comparing schedules. The shuffling of feet resumed.

By the end of the day, it seemed I'd been in school for months. Senior year promised no more than earlier years had delivered. Nothing had changed over the summer. Maybe that was my fault. I was idle when I should've labored over self-improvements. I watched workers drive their trucks and I read library books teachers hadn't assigned. Nothing more. Like Charley, I should've studied fashion magazines, memorized the latest makeup shades and hairstyles, prepared myself for the possibilities of senior year.

※ ※ ※

That afternoon, at home, I was on my last slice of apple when my mother remembered Elissa. "Did you see her?"

Here it came. My mother was always after me to share stuff and didn't want to accept that I wasn't the sharing type. I kept much of what I thought or felt inside, safe from everyone, but also knew how to say enough to keep myself out of trouble. "She's in all my classes," I said. Was I lucky or cursed? Being with Elissa that much had given me an opportunity to study her. Charley had been right about the ashen skin undisguised by makeup. *This is who I am*, her face said. *I no longer have any need to pretend to be what I am not. All pretense has been shocked out of me.* My mother didn't need to know any of this.

"I hope you were friendly. Said hello."

"Nobody says hello in class," I said.

"Then afterwards. When you were walking down the hall." She was desperate for signs of social aptitude on my part, even if it involved an insane classmate.

"There wasn't any chance to talk."

"You mustn't ignore her. That would be the worst thing, to ignore her."

How would my mother know anything about the desires of a girl just released from Pineville? Maybe being ignored was exactly what Elissa wanted. "She's in my classes. That's all. We don't hang out together."

"You'll feel bad if she ends up back in the hospital and you never said a friendly word, not even one hello." She carried my plate to the sink. "You'd feel bad about that. I know you."

She didn't know me at all, but I knew enough not to say that.

On the porch, I sat with a World History assignment. An empty truck sped past. Eugene ran along the edge of the ditch, pumping his arm frantically, but there wasn't any horn blast of recognition. The rejection, if that's what it was, had no effect on my brother, who still zigzagged across the ditch, jumping from the roadside to our yard, back and forth, back and forth.

The next driver was friendlier or more attentive, honking loudly in answer to Eugene's gyrations, but that didn't stop the zigzagging either. When you're ten, you are who you are and that's all. No one studies you, trying to detect signs that you're the person they suspected all along. Or not. When she was ten, no one guessed Elissa would be shut away in Pineville in a few years.

Every day that first week, she wore the same beige jumper, though she changed her blouse. She never wore makeup and, as I'd predicted, sat at the rejects' table. Vicky, leader if rejects can be said to have a leader, fidgeted with her food and forgot to go back for seconds the first day Elissa joined them. But when you've been cast out by most of your classmates, maybe casting out someone else isn't easy. Secretly, I admired Vicky. For myself, if I'd been relegated to that table, I would've seized the opportunity to exclude Elissa, announcing to the cafeteria that here, at last, was someone beneath me in life's caste system.

The next week, the jumper was navy. The week after that, black. Then the beige reappeared and it seemed Elissa's wardrobe had shrunk in proportion to her mind, which surely must feel substantially diminished now that all those mad thoughts had been shocked out of it.

We all watched her. Elissa was the only crazy person we knew and had earned our constant attention. She might, any moment, do something to demand a return to Pineville. None of us wanted to miss the instant when that happened. And so we watched her. The way she walked to her locker with a slow, careful gait while others sprinted past. The way she stacked her belongings neatly while the rest of us crammed notebooks and test papers, unwashed gym socks and half-eaten sandwiches into our lockers. The way she smiled before answering a question, in class or out, as if she knew the question was a ploy masking the real concerns. Are you still crazy? How did you get that way? Do you see signs that one day we will be the crazy ones, the ones people can't stop staring at? If she knew the answers to questions we didn't ask, she never said.

By the end of September, workers reached our house. They gouged chunks of earth from both our property and our neighbor's across the street, widening the lanes until the road was no longer recognizable as the one where I'd always lived. Then they scraped and leveled, preparing for layers of dirt and gravel, followed by asphalt. In the afternoon, when the bus dropped me off, grime obliterated the men's features, hiding who they were from everyone.

Our house had always sat back, aloof from the occasional car or truck driving past. Now it was pushed forward, calling bold attention to itself. You wouldn't think just repositioning the road several yards closer would have such a profound effect, but it did. Widening the lanes made the road more of a presence and reduced our house from what it had once been.

In early October, Elissa and I were partnered in English class. The assignment was to select scenes from *Hamlet*, illustrate them, and write short narrative explanations. We'd read the play and discussed what Mrs. Cormier considered significant, and she should know, having taught senior English practically since the school was built. Her course always began with poetry by the Brownings, then moved to Shakespeare. She wasn't rearranging that syllabus, its worth proven over these many years, just because a crazy girl happened to be in her class.

For a short while that morning, Mrs. Cormier's room came alive. Students wandered happily, trying to decide whether their assigned partner should move or they should. If the person next to your partner wasn't moving, where would you sit? And if the person next to you didn't move, same problem for your partner. The whole process demanded extensive conversations about who was moving where. Much too complex to resolve in a single class period. Mrs. Cormier disagreed, intervening as needed, directing students here and there. Desks scraped the floor as they were rearranged. Elissa sat quietly through the chaos and gave no signs of joining me, so I was forced to move to her back corner. When she saw me approaching, she did turn her desk to face the empty one next to it.

When I passed Charley, she put a finger to her throat, pretending to gag.

"Any ideas?" I asked Elissa, my text open to the first page of the play.

She smiled, then said, "Ophelia. Everyone expects me to choose Ophelia."

Her directness unnerved me more than the accuracy of the observation. "No one expects anything." I denied what we both knew.

"They expect me to act like a lunatic. To drown myself like Ophelia." She glanced around the room as if receiving confirmation from the faces she glimpsed. "Drowning is awful, don't you think? I'd never drown myself."

I imagined her in that tub of water and blood. No one would want to drown in her own blood. I understood that quite well. "We don't have to do Ophelia," I said, hoping she didn't guess what I was thinking. "What about the gravediggers? With Halloween stuff everywhere, we could pick up skulls easy."

"They'd all be so disappointed." She said this in the exaggerated manner of a performer on stage, but I was the only one to notice.

"It's just another stupid Cormier assignment," I said. "Nobody cares what we do."

"We'll do the part where they find Ophelia, floating. Dead."
She smiled as if the image pleased her. Someone else drowning
didn't bother her.

"We don't have to," I said. "Really." I waited, but she said
nothing. Just kept smiling. "Okay, okay," I said as if we'd been
arguing. "We'll do Ophelia. But we have to do two scenes, not just
the drowning one."

Elissa didn't object and we spent the rest of the period planning a diorama.

The warning bell rang and everyone returned to their own
desks. Charley leaned forward, her chair directly behind mine,
and whispered, her lips brushing my hair. "Did she say anything
weird? I bet Suzanna that she said tons of weird things."

I didn't answer, only twitched my shoulders. Mrs. Cormier
stood at the front of the room, giving additional instructions. My
twitches could've meant anything. Charley had to make of them
what she would.

During assembly, homecoming court was announced, beginning with the single girl the freshman class was allowed and working up to the senior class with its six allotted slots, reward for years
of devotion to education, or so Mr. Gutierrez claimed. Charley
thought she had a chance. So did I. Finally, there was room for
only two more seniors. One was Charley, now fully transformed.
She covered her face with both hands, mimicking other girls whose
names were called before hers. The second name had to be another
senior and could be my name. Mr. Gutierrez cleared his throat.
Say my name. My name. Mine. No one remembered lessons from
the first day of school.

"Yvette Meche," he announced, disregarding the silent pleas
telepathed to him by nearly every unnamed senior girl in that auditorium. Lessons remembered.

"I was hoping you'd make it too," Charley said as we waited
for dismissal from the auditorium.

"That would've been the shock of the hour," I said, trying not
to sound bitter, then added, before Charley could protest, "I knew
you'd get it. Never a doubt."

She grinned, happy to hear me echoing her own cheerful as-
sumption.

"Maybe you'll win," I said, though I couldn't muster enough
belief to sound convincing.

"Maybe," Charley said, without a hint of skepticism. The wonders of standing firmly on a higher rung of the popularity ladder. She turned to accept congratulations from two senior girls sitting behind us. "I'm in total shock is the thing," she said. "I didn't think I had a chance. I was sure it was going to be one of you guys." Surely those seniors smelled the insincerity on her breath, but they didn't make any accusations. The first rule a girl learns is the popular ones are always gracious, at least publicly.

By the time we crept out of the auditorium and stopped at our lockers, the warning bell was ringing for fifth period. Chemistry. That was my only class where seats were assigned and Elissa couldn't appropriate the farthest desk as her own, as she had in every other class. Mrs. Domingue believed students couldn't memorize the Periodic Table when distracted by the proximity of friends.

Elissa sat in the front center of the room, strategically placed where she could be constantly scrutinized. Mrs. Domingue didn't want a psycho leaping into madness during a crucial step in a chemistry experiment.

I sat in the second row, diagonal from Elissa so I had a clear view of her. When chemistry grew too boring, an almost daily occurrence, I studied Elissa for signs of reversion to the completely mad girl lurking beneath her placid surface. Today, she seemed paler than usual. Was she nursing a resentment or disappointment? Had she anticipated selection to the homecoming court? Surely not. And yet hadn't I held my own breath before that last name was called, the name I knew could never be mine?

Sunlight fell from the high windows and slashed across Elissa's desk. Mrs. Domingue droned about the interaction of this chemical with that one and the necessity for vigilance and caution in the experiment she outlined. We students stared at her in a stupor, confident someone else must be paying careful attention so one of us would know how to avoid catastrophe.

Elissa sighed, her chest rising then falling dramatically, enough to give even Mrs. Domingue pause. "Questions, so far?" Elissa wasn't easy to ignore, but Mrs. Domingue deliberately avoided looking at her. If she'd wanted, Elissa could've reached out a hand and jabbed Mrs. Domingue's protruding belly.

Again, Elissa sighed, this time even more dramatically than the first. No one in the room moved, each of us secretly thrilled to be present at what might prove to be the first sign of her latest descent into lunacy.

"Elissa, dear, do you have a question?" Mrs. Domingue sounded exhausted. Having a crazy girl in your classroom was tiring. "Well?" she pressed when Elissa's smile wasn't followed by an answer.

In the back of the room, the place Elissa longed to be, someone rapped a pencil against the edge of a desk. Rap, rap, rap, the only sound in that science room. The beam of light had moved and now hovered directly over Elissa's head. She could've been an angel or a saint.

"If you don't have a question, pay attention." This was as patient as Mrs. Domingue got. There was a limit as to how far teachers pushed Elissa, the only student certifiably crazy among all of us.

Elissa did not, as anyone else would've, protest she'd already been paying very close attention. Instead, she unfolded a paper clip and began meticulously poking tiny holes in paper she'd used for notes. If she'd been anybody else, Mrs. Domingue would've harangued her for most of the remaining period about defacing property, being inattentive and disrespectful, the cost of school supplies, on and on and on. But a reputation for insanity has its advantages and one of them is that people are afraid of being the one to push you over the edge where you balance precariously. So, Elissa poked and Mrs. Domingue attended to the intricacies of chemical interactions.

When Eugene called me to the phone one more time that night, I expected Charley's voice. She'd already called twice for advice on the color of her homecoming formal, but any excuse to talk about her new status would do. Maybe now the topic was the one she'd mentioned that afternoon, wearing a hat to the football game. Some girls did and others didn't. Should she? How was I supposed to know?

"Hey," I said, trying to disguise my annoyance. Surely there was a limit as to how supportive I had to be.

"My mother says you can come home with me tomorrow after school so we can finish our project."

"What?" I was abrupt with confusion.

"If you don't want to come over, that's okay. I understand."

I pictured the smile, no lipstick on the mouth lifted at the corners like everyone else's smile and yet not like anyone else's at all.

"I didn't say that." I wasn't letting anyone accuse me of being rude to a girl just out of Pineville. "I have to check with my mom is all." At that, my mother glanced up from her magazine. "See if she can pick me up from your house." I added, for my eavesdropping mother's benefit, "If I had my own car, it wouldn't be a problem at all."

"My mother can bring you home." Her eagerness surprised me. "My mother said that, said she could bring you home afterwards."

Naturally, my mother was delighted, insisted on speaking with Elissa's mother to offer her own driving services. She'd be happy to pick me up, save Mrs. Barberot the trouble. "It's lovely of Elissa to think of this," my mother said. I couldn't hear Mrs. Barberot's end of the conversation, but she must've insisted on doing the driving and then reminded my mom about the English project. "Yes, yes, I know. But this will also give the girls a chance to visit. You know how girls are." She frowned, remembering Mrs. Barberot had little experience with what normal girls might like to do, and hung up as quickly as manners allowed.

I called Charley, pleased to offer a different topic of conversation. But after directing me to observe everything closely, most especially everything in Elissa's room, she was back on homecoming. I gave a few grunts in response to her descriptions of dresses she was considering, but she either didn't notice or didn't mind my lack of enthusiasm. One less rival for the sweetheart competitions in the spring. What club in its right mind would choose a sweetheart as indifferent as me?

The next morning, I was ready early, so I sat on the front porch to wait for the bus. My father had already left for work and my mother was occupied with Eugene, making sure he had lunch money, homework, and a permission slip she'd signed after supper last night. My brother only bothered remembering what he considered important and nothing connected with school ever made his list.

I liked being alone outside in the quiet. Dew still glistened on blades of grass and a red sun hung low in the east. Other than a few bird chirps, an occasional truck was the only disturbance.

Workers were spreading dirt and gravel and preparing the roadbed about half a mile away. They progressed in shifts, first digging and widening and leveling a section of road, then returning to dump dirt and gravel, then coming back a third and fourth time to pave first one side, then the other. Our section, already dug and widened, would be paved within the week. Then our family would no longer be isolated, but connected to the main highway, the same as nearly everyone else I knew.

All day, in each class, Elissa eyed me. In chemistry, she turned twice, as if to make sure I was still there. But she didn't say anything or make any move in my direction, my presence being assurance enough. I wondered whether Charley or anyone else caught those looks. No one said anything, so I guessed not. Charley joined a lunch table of homecoming court girls to discuss what they were wearing so no one's outfit clashed with anyone else's or, worse, duplicated what someone else wore. Charley was too preoccupied to notice anyone watching me.

After final dismissal, she found me at my locker. "Don't forget. I want to hear all the gruesome details."

I shoved Chemistry into the back of my locker, pulled out World History and French.

Charley slouched against lockers next to mine, reached out a hand to tug my sleeve. "Remember."

"Okay, okay." I slammed the locker door, making more noise than I'd intended, but no one turned in my direction. At this time of day, sounds swallowed each other.

"Call me the minute you get home," she said, then left for her own locker upstairs, directly above my own.

Elissa waited on the front steps, but gave no signs of impatience and didn't seem particularly eager for my company. She didn't say anything as we walked towards the bus line. Too much silence makes me nervous, so I talked about our classes and asked a few questions to which she gave one-word answers. Yes, history had too much homework. Yes, our math teacher would look better with a beard disguising his weak chin. Maybe I'd imagined she was directing extraordinary attention to me all day. Her lethargic responses definitely suggested otherwise.

On the bus, she took the window seat, always preferable, and left me with the aisle. During the short ride, she looked out the window and remained silent. I didn't try to start up a conversation either, piqued she hadn't offered me the choice spot. When a boy I recognized as a junior looked my way, I pulled out my French workbook and pretended to concentrate on that.

At her house, Elissa's mother waited with fresh apple pie, vanilla ice cream, and café au lait. The kitchen smelled like a bakery. Still, I could tell right away Elissa's mother was a hoverer, worse than my own and that was saying something. I constantly complained about my mother driving me crazy. Most of the girls I knew had the same complaints about their mothers, but going crazy had only actually happened to Elissa.

"So, how was school today, girls?" her mother asked, sounding exactly like my own.

I waited for Elissa to answer. When she didn't, I said, "Same as always." I paused, again waiting for something from Elissa. "We have tons of homework in French. Don't you think?"

"Tons," she repeated. Even crazy girls pick up their cues sometimes.

"I'll clear those dishes, if you're done," Mrs. Barberot said. Everything in the kitchen sparkled. White appliances. White walls. White linoleum speckled with bits of gold and emerald. Copper pans lining one wall, silver serving spoons another.

I knew the rest of the house would prove as immaculate and also knew how Mrs. Barberot spent her days while Elissa was in school, what she'd done when Elissa was locked away.

"You can work here or in the den. Wherever you think best." She ran water over our dishes in the sink and, with the faucet still running, returned to pass a sponge over the spotless table.

"Our stuff is in my bedroom," Elissa said.

"Shall I move it?" Mrs. Barberot's desire to have us in an open area where she could watch over us was too transparent.

I looked down at the table, embarrassed for Elissa and for her mother too.

"We'll start in the bedroom. Move to the table later, if we need more room." Elissa stood, turned to me. For support?

"Sounds good." I picked up my backpack from the floor next to my chair. This kitchen didn't tolerate even temporary clutter.

"We'll need scissors," Elissa said.

"Scissors?" Her mother's voice rose, either in surprise or alarm.

"To cut out our pictures and captions."

"Right," her mother said.

Elissa's bedroom was nearly as sterile as the kitchen. A pink chenille spread covered a twin bed and three dark brown teddy bears sat at soldierly attention on the pillows. A desk in one corner held neatly arranged pens and pencils, stapler and paper clips, colored markers. The walls were bare, giving no hints of belonging to anyone in particular. Even my walls had a couple of abstract posters, described by my mother as not what girls usually liked. Why didn't I have movie stars on my walls like other girls? She was an expert on girls and if I could only be like them, my mother'd be a happy woman. Not much to ask, she thought. Impossible, I thought.

While I occupied myself cutting pictures with the scissors Mrs. Barberot supplied, Elissa sat at her desk writing out our narratives. I tried to think of something to say, but her back didn't invite small talk.

When she was done, she brought her strips of paper for inspection. "Your handwriting is awesome," I said and I wasn't just trying to make her feel good. Her words flowed across light green strips of construction paper. "Where did you learn to write that way? Especially the capitals?" The letters curled and twisted as if a professional calligrapher had shaped them.

"I had a class," she said. "They're always wanting you to take a class."

"Who?" As soon as the word left my mouth, I recognized my mistake.

She smiled. "The doctors. The nurses. The counselors. All of them." She picked up one of our Ophelias, a girl in a white nightgown who'd been sleeping on a mattress before I cut her out. "If you take a class, you're getting better. That's what they all think." She tore off a corner of Ophelia's nightgown, but the tiny defect was invisible unless you inspected carefully. Mrs. Cormier would never notice.

"So you took classes," I said. Here was something I fully understood. Even at Pineville there was a way to fit in, a way not to. And of course Elissa, when she was able, chose the easy way, fitting in at least on the surface, presenting a calm and studious exterior to the world.

"Most of them were a bore, but the writing one was okay. I liked having a different handwriting to use whenever I wanted."

"A disguise."

She grinned and didn't look crazy at all. "Right," she said. "A disguise."

We worked quickly then and when we finished both scenes, I stepped back to survey the finished product. "Looks good, don't you think?"

She tilted her head to one side, reviewing the two halves of our display. On the one side, Ophelia stood with her father. On the other, she floated, eyes closed, appearing too content to be dead, but that was the fault of the mattress our Ophelia had advertised. Nothing we could do about that. Elissa glanced at the open door. "I'm wearing something special the day of our report." She glanced at the door again. "Want to see?"

"Sure."

She stepped into her closet and, in a minute, emerged in a floor-length white cotton gown. Her eyelids were half shut, her lips painted pale pink and parted.

I should've told her pale lipsticks were passé. Instead, I said, "Looks good, but I don't think Mrs. Cormier wants costumes." Elissa was my partner for this report and I didn't want anyone laughing at her or, worse, not laughing at all.

"I'm wearing this." She took one step towards me, then another, then stopped. "Everyone expects me to."

I said nothing as I gathered paper and cardboard remnants and tossed them into the trashcan next to her desk.

"Here." Elissa held out an identical white gown. Was it from Pineville? "For you."

"Me?"

She didn't smile or offer an answer, just held my gaze with her own.

I shook my head, but even as I did, reached for the gown, slipped it over my sweater and jeans. We stood side by side, reflected in the full-length mirror attached to her closet door. In our identical gowns, we looked enough alike to be sisters.

"You girls did a great job." Mrs. Barberot smiled at me from the doorway and looked so grateful, I blushed. She didn't mention the gowns we wore. Maybe Elissa spent every afternoon discarding her drab school uniform for something else. Maybe she changed several times daily and her mother was accustomed to this and would've been surprised if we still wore the outfits she'd seen earlier.

"We're done with the scissors." Elissa handed two pairs to her mother. "You want them back. Right?"

Her mother bent her neck, a flower wilting on its stem, to stare at the scissors Elissa placed in her hands. After a moment, she said, "If you want more pie, just let me know."

Elissa closed the door gently, then waited until her mother's footsteps faded. "She keeps the scissors and knives locked in a kitchen drawer. She also locks the bathroom medicine cabinet. She's afraid I'm still crazy."

"Are you?"

She shrugged. "Who knows?"

I returned the gown before leaving.

Maybe Mrs. Barberot always drove fast, but I suspected Elissa's insistence on staying home with her French homework caused today's speed. We flew from her house to mine and when we arrived, I was surprised to discover construction completed. The workers had moved on to the next strip, leaving the road in front of my house paved, exactly like the roads most people lived on. Having watched the process, I knew the asphalt masked gravel and dirt, but the smooth outer layer gave no hints of that ragged underside.

"Come over any time," Mrs. Barberot, oblivious to my surprise, said. "I can always drive you home."

I hurried out of the car, backpack in hand. "Thanks." She could interpret that answer as she wished.

My mother and her questions waited in the kitchen, but I rushed past her to the bathroom where she wouldn't follow. I ran the faucet, looked at myself in the mirror. Nothing new. The same me as always.

That night, getting ready to shave my legs, I pulled my razor from the cabinet, dumped the used blade in the trash and reached for a replacement. As the tub filled, I weighed the shiny metal, surprisingly flimsy, in one hand. Had Elissa bothered with a new blade or made do with an old one? When I passed the sharp edge across my left wrist, it was cool and even when I pressed as hard as possible without breaking skin, I didn't sense any danger or threat. I studied my mirrored reflection. No changes, still. What had been her last thought before the cut? That no one could expect anything from her now? I turned from the mirror and made myself concentrate on centering the blade in my razor. Then I stepped into the full tub and submerged until only my face was exposed, the rest of me hidden below the surface of water, rising and falling in miniature waves as I moved one leg, then an arm, then something else.

from *Eliza: The New Orleans Years, 1837-1862*

Papa Had Pulled Us Down, Preaching Hellfire Out of the Flask of His Mind

He was the vicar, but he was a slurry
disgrace. He'd reel and stutter, even weep,
and when the deacon tripped over him, stone-
cold in the nave, we wept, we prayed, we buried
him, engaged passage—and sailed. I slept at sea,
as sound as Maria and little Louise.
Mum on deck stuffed with sweets and tea.
And the captain—what did he want from me?
My red hair. My fair skin. I was listless,
losing horizons. He held me steady,
touched my sleeve. Like Papa he wore mutton chops.
I wed at sea while my sisters slept, tucked in.

My Captain Sets Sail

I stand on the levee, slapping at gnats
with my glove, air so thick I barely inhale.

And there on the quay—that man. The one who touched
my sleeve. I lift my fan to shield my cheeks.

What does he dare imagine? I'm pouring tears
of absence? I'll weep when my husband returns!

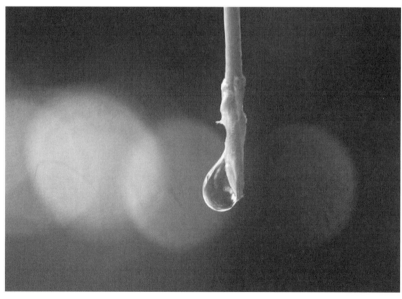

Jen Hoppa, photograph

Bonsoir Danse, Soleil Couché

Goodbye dance, the sun is asleep.
  —slaves singing as they leave Congo Square
  on Sunday—free day—before 9 p.m. curfew

I slip like a wild thing into the street.
The very earth pulses and thrums with the beat
of hollow-log drums, the fling of tambourines.
Slaves raising Cain. There go the ones from Tremé—
free men of colour, heading for Congo Square.
Perhaps my captain is already there,
pinching the ginger cakes—you catch what I mean.
He'll weave home. Tease me with sleeves of pralines.
But, wait, I've gone too far. Alone. And who,
who is that staring at me? I look for shade.
Those drums . . . my whole body humming . . .

In the French Market

I walk as fast as I can, threading the stalls.
Acorn squash, late potatoes weigh my basket,
anything to roast on the grate. Yams. Cushaw.

He's here. I finger a sprig of sassafras.
That man . . . called Caleb. I am unreeling
beneath the surface, so deep I cannot breathe.

I grip my shawl. *I'll leave. Yes.* A girl glides by
with macaroons and nougat, oranges, candied
pecans. He sidles beside, drops a silver

into the *marchande*'s hand, bows to me with *figues
celestes*, sweet figs from heaven. Anyone can
see. I do not turn. I stand. I eat. I feast.

Tamsen Donner

*One of the death-stricken at Donner Lake may have said, with
tremulous voice: 'Look! There, just above us, is a beautiful house.'*
—C. F. McGlashan,
History of the Donner Party

Frontier

Dear Sister, our house is made of hides
lashed to branches; it tips in the gusts
and down come the Bible and ladle,

four tea cups, the children's stiff rag dolls, all
from the mantle of ice, and up again

when the wind dies and I set it to rights
and turn back to kettle and coaxing the fire,

pouring the endless weak brew gone
half-cold before it meets their blue lips.

How quickly the warmth is snuffed out of all things,

how grateful we are for our chores.

The children progress in their lessons.
At daybreak, the fine winter sun
lights the veins in the walls,
and their faces, crept over by frost.

Slates

In the first fortnight, dear Sister, I dreamt the farm and cursed our guts and in moments of fugue would hum in the pantry while taking down foodstuffs, for instance, or sweeping the floor. I would hear the scratching of its straws, so real was the sensation. Or, I would rush through the front rooms, turning the shutter-cranks to drive out the cold. Then know myself as suddenly to be kneeling on the hardened snow, writing the children's lesson in a steady hand.

I Wake in the Night

Dearest, it is lightless without hope
of wick or flint, and so brutal
the cold that I am quite senseless of their bodies
beside mine—mine?
Mine is pain without body. Are these blankets?
Are these my children, their seizing breaths
evidence of my own form?

On the Death of Our Trusted Dog, Uno

My only S., it was one of the ox-hands who asked —
he came to me ashamed — Ma'am, he said — what sort of name is that
for a creature as myself — when I had thought of it, myself — first
two weeks ago? — The only decorum I requested: — In the woods,
where the children do not venture, and away
from their ears — He was allowed, at home, to sprawl
before the hearth — The wedding china from Boston,
the full-blown roses.

Sister, Keep My Memory in Your House

What am I to you but nearly forgotten — the reflection of your skirts
on the polished floor — you roam the halls with purpose, the ring of keys
at your waist — The girl in the kitchen in your mended blue —
her eyes are narrow, covetous
— take care.

Our lessons, our hoops, our tightly woven hair — Sundays
bent over embroidery and verse after verse —

There was a time we imagined it — the girls and the boys
in their rough quarters — the girls in our mended dresses, the girls and their boys
in the fields

although we never spoke it, although we lay as near to one flesh
beneath the quilts in winter, the lamp oil singeing the glassed air.

The Skeleton

My witness. It was all was left
after we scraped the hair from the hides
and tore them in stripes
and boiled them to paste

—a tracery of branches useless
against the snow. We wake at night
and shake ourselves and sleep and wake
to grind the skins between our teeth.

Do you recall our meager girlhood?
The dull winters, the coarse meal
bubbling long on the fire, somewhere in the pot
a dice of bacon chased
by the long-handled spoon?

How do we swallow now?
We eat the skins; the last a lap-robe
with rot in the fringe; it had been the door.

No door, no roof, no sound but snow,
no light but from the coals
beneath the kettle, no souls but these,
fed by the hide, shaking within the house of sticks
that is no shelter.

Foxes in the Snow

It is our impulse, Sister,
to curl around what ember
remains, unlike these creatures
so brave of the cold and
all through the ordeal fearless
of us, yipping on the rocks
above our heads their ribs
girded in ice these beauties
who look me in the eye unlike
the reverend who blushed when
I confessed the feeling of spirit
leaving body during certain hymns
and you laughed at me in the
carriage home because I was
too thin and given to strong
emotion and you couldn't fathom
the desire to leave
your plump trappings —

and the mornings I rose
early and walked the fields where
the foxes knew to fear us and
I wanted keenly to touch them to
be fox or wind or long grass, not
a human girl — and how

it grieves me now to think of rising
and pinning my hair, the heavy
oak bedstead, our thick flannel gowns
and the piano alone in the parlor because
it was not only that spectral line
that tied me, but these things, your dear face
grumbling inside your tilted bonnet
about the long cold service, our steaming
feet by the fire and

there was never, truly, the wish
to leave entirely, only

to be nearer
those things that escaped me,
Sister.

Zac King, photograph

Welded in Beijing, 1989

Were this all just about a weld, the metal
would snap in response to the hot hit, zzzzzzzet,
   fuse hard to itself, then become cold.
We would hear the yellow cobra buzz
   repeat and snap again and again.
The iron would sing about yielding into one.

Were this all just about a weld, the tool's
twisting reptile cord would coil and dance,
then stiffen and jump as the hot, hissing
charge rushed through the line seeking cold steel.
The white-hot weld, molten and aglow for a second,
would make sure the blue fit gave no resistance.

It would fix it firmly.

Were this all just about a weld, in the morning
the metal would lie stiff on the walk,
motionless, fashioned a weld at a time into a
welcoming gate, a fence or a protective door.

But it is not. This is more about just shredding,
   and crushing, and angrily ripping apart.
This is all about muzzles striking lasers at midnight.
This is all about man-cobras spitting, washing
   the dust from the wings of a thousand
   little white-shirted butterflies.
This is all about being twisted by tank cleats.
This is all about ten words for death written
   in the night air by tracer arcs spat from rifles
This is all about nervous hope, a wanting to weld
   sprung steel back into place.

Now, there are bicycles twisted hard on the pavement.
Now, there are bodies twisted soft in the lanes and doorways.

The metal forms rigor, stacked motionless on the pavement,
   slung over and over by cobras at Tian'anmen.

A white priming will not hide their hideous weld wounds
nor remove the red stains dropped onto their stretchers.

137

Holes
(or Annotated Scrapbook, Sections Slightly Charred)

Photo #1 (from personal archives) —Most of my face. All of my nose but only my right eye. Too much of my hair. The new perm makes me look like a poodle.

Photo #2 (from personal archives) —My right hand with the quarter-inch hole in the center, between the bones of my ring and middle fingers.

Photo #3 (from personal archives) —My left hand, a mirror image of the right.

It's my first new camera in years and I have to test it out so I'm taking pictures of myself, the stuff in my apartment, and my hands. I had the holes made in them ten years ago. I was sure I'd earn more than two hundred a week traveling as The Fountain Woman.

❈   ❈   ❈

Newspaper photograph dated 15 March — The place where our trailer stood. Blackened cement block foundation, some of the charred metal shell, a few spindly trees in the background. Caption: "Local family meets with devastation."

I decided to get the holes made the year after my folks' trailer caught fire, or rather exploded, because of a leak in the propane tank. Least that's what the propane company said. They claimed it was a hardware problem, but I think it was because someone forgot to seal the tank properly when they'd delivered propane earlier in the afternoon. After the explosion there was little we could do to prove that, because there was nothing left. The trailer was gone. Or, more precisely, in little pieces scattered over a quarter-mile radius.

We moved into a new trailer two and a half blocks from the old one. Smoke-stained kitchen utensils, clothing, and photo album pages came back to us over a period of months. Every other day we'd get a pair of socks or a sweater, a couple of butter knives, and a few sooty pictures. We washed the clothes, scoured the dishes and silverware, and I spent evenings going over the pictures with a kneadable eraser from the art supply store, trying to get off more soot.

❄ ❄ ❄

Polaroid snapshot taken by my mother of my father sitting on the brown corduroy living room couch that we got from the Salvation Army (the cushions smelled faintly of sour apples). He wears a red sweatshirt and sweatpants, eats a powdered sugar donut, and has white flecks trailing down the front of his shirt.

Three weeks after the first trailer blew up and two weeks after we'd moved into the new one, my father went crazy. He refused to eat anything but donuts and orange drink, stopped talking in the mornings and didn't say much in the evenings, and refused to go to the paperclip and thumbtack factory with my mother. They'd met there, both worked in quality control.

"Please," said my mother to my father every morning while I ate cornflakes. "You have to get dressed."

My father smiled at my mother's request like she'd complimented his hair, and turned back to the morning news programs. I don't think he watched the shows as much as he stared at the moving mouths, the business suits, and the cheery expressions of the anchor people. Something about them, their orderly happiness, calmed him.

At the factory my mother opened every hundred-and-fiftieth box of clips or tacks and counted the number to make sure the machines were accurate. Often she came home with Band-Aids on her thumbs. My father made sure the thumbtacks had points and the paperclips were bent correctly. He liked the exactness of his job, the scales he used to be certain the right amount of metal was being used in each paperclip and tack.

My mother took the Polaroid picture hoping that if my father saw himself he'd come to his senses. He nodded at the photo and took another bite of his donut.

I was eighteen and had already decided to save my family by getting holes in my hands.

❄ ❄ ❄

Grainy black-and-white novelty postcard, charred slightly in the lower left corner, of my grandfather. He is young, maybe twenty-five, wears a short-sleeved white shirt and long black pants. He sits in a wooden chair, his hands tight against the chair arms, as blurry streams of water shoot up through the holes in his palms. White lettering under his picture: "The Fantastic Human Fountain."

There are two different stories about how my grandfather got the holes in his hands, but both of them involve his horsing around with a cousin while drinking bootleg whiskey and staking tomatoes in the garden. In one story the cousin pounded a metal stake through my grandfather's hand on a dare. In the other they were fencing and my grandfather fell down, tried to use the stake to support himself. The stake went between two bones in his hand in just the right place, left a hole the surgeon kept open with a surgical stainless steel tube. Legend has it my grandfather was still kind of drunk when he told the surgeon to do this, but he was also remembering the carnival that had been through town two months earlier, and perhaps already dreaming up his act as the human fountain.

My grandfather had a somewhat reputable surgeon make the matching hole in his right hand and insert another stainless steel tube. The wooden chair, his only prop, had hoses running up through the arms. Grandpa made good money on the circuit but left after ten years and returned to farming. He died in a combine accident when my dad was twenty-seven, five years before I was born.

"Sideshow life was probably safer than life on a farm," my dad often said when I was young. "I think he wished he would have stayed there."

"Craziness," said my mother and shook her head. "It wouldn't have been the place to raise a family."

My father shrugged. I think he would've preferred life in a sideshow to life working in a factory, but he was never one to say what was on his mind. This might account for the fact that, rather than say anything about the trailer exploding, he decided it would be easier to go crazy.

✿   ✿   ✿

Polaroid snapshot of used beige Ford station wagon with brown Naugahyde seats and pink plastic beads hanging from rearview mirror. Sleeping bag, tent, two grocery bags of snacks, one pot, a cooking spoon, two gallons of water, and camp stove are not entirely visible but all piled in back seat.

When I decided to get the holes made I was thinking of the lost trailer, thinking of fountains, thinking of water, even though

water wouldn't have helped the trailer explosion. I bought the
station wagon cheap, planned to travel and be the second human fountain in our family, have appearances at tattoo parlors
and carnivals, send money home to my folks in Ohio. This way
they wouldn't have to feed me, and I figured they could use the
extra cash, what with my dad going crazy and all. I didn't tell my
mother about my plan to get the holes, just said that I would be on
the road for the summer, working in a funnel-cake booth at county
fairs.

"I don't like the thought of you running all over the country
like that," she said. "It's not safe." She unloaded a bag of groceries, including boxes of donuts for my dad.

"I want to save for college," I told her. A black lie, but one
that would pacify her.

"College," she said, setting the sixth box of donuts on the
table. She and my father had wanted me to take classes at the local
community college in the fall, but when the trailer exploded, their
extra money went with it.

"Maybe graphic design or something," I told her because she
always said I was good at art, but I hated drawing, even if I wasn't
bad at it. I felt worse for my parents than I did for myself about
the college money. They loved me. I wanted to help them.

"In September," she said and nodded. Her words were blessing enough for me to leave, even though I planned to be traveling in the fall. I knew I was not a college sort of person, but my
mother never believed this. I figured since she gave birth to me, it
was her right to pretend I was who she wanted me to be, and my
duty not to object too loudly while going my own way.

❆ ❆ ❆

*Color photograph from ten-year-old newspaper advertisement.
Cream-colored brick building with sign over the front door:* Piercings and
Tattoos. *Heavy burgundy curtains are in the windows on either side of the
door, along with two empty chairs on raised platforms.*

I took pictures of my grandfather to the piercing salon,
photos of him and my father when Dad was ten, holding a hose up
to Grandpa's hand and shooting a stream of water through. The
fellow who owned the salon was Indian, claimed to be a fakir who
had pierced the hands and feet of other fakirs. He didn't have

holes in his own hands, but there were black-and-white pictures all over the walls, photos of him with swords and nails sticking out of his arms. His face was wrinkled enough to make him about seventy-five, but his hands looked young, free of the raised veins and knobbed knuckles usually associated with age. The fakir nodded at the pictures of my grandfather, said the operation would be free if I'd agree to be on display while I healed.

"Been a long time since I performed one of these," he told me. "They went out of style some years ago. If you were to sit in the window for a few days, be on display, I'd consider the bill paid in full."

I don't remember the operation, just that when I came to my hands hurt and were swathed in bandages. The pain was less than I expected, but I spent three days in a haze, drinking some sort of black tea through a straw from a flowered china cup. The fakir was a pleasant gentleman and a good cook who fed me curried rice and lentils and told me not to move my hands too much or too quickly. In the end I had to believe that he was a real fakir, or a real something-or-other, because on the third day, when the bandages came off so he could show me how to turn and clean the metal posts, there was almost no swelling or redness. He'd inserted quarter-inch stainless steel tubes between the bones of my ring and middle fingers. I had to turn them around once each day, a full turn, and clean them with alcohol. After a week my hands were nearly healed. I don't think the body does that normally. The fakir gave me pink plastic plugs to keep in the holes when I wanted them to be less noticeable.

❖   ❖   ❖

Polaroid of me and a seventy-year-old tattooed lady standing outside a tattoo parlor in Memphis, taken right after she told me I should have been born fifty years earlier. The rest of the pictures from this trip were lost when someone swiped my camera.

I drove through Cleveland and worked a few days at a fair just outside of Akron, spent time in Philadelphia and Louisville at tattoo parlors, then went down to Orlando and New Orleans. At first I was the Human Fountain and shot water through the holes, usually with a hose, but that bored people quickly. I thought up other little tricks, like putting a straw through my hand and drinking out of a glass, or fitting a pen or pencil through and writing my name. A few times I smoked a cigarette through the hole, but I quit that one after I got burned. I spent most of my time in small towns along the way, got gigs at county fairs and in tattoo parlors. The owners usually gave me food and a place to sleep as long as I'd hang out and answer questions asked by customers.

I called my mom every week from a pay phone, told her where I was and that the funnel-cake booth was doing well. She sounded tired but pleased to hear from me, never mentioned my dad unless I asked.

"He's doing well enough," she said, which I figured to mean that he was still alive and watching television and eating donuts.

I liked traveling, but there were snags. The station wagon's front windshield began leaking during a rainstorm in Texas and the back windshield was quick to follow. The back seat smelled musty for the rest of the trip, no matter how much baking soda I poured on it. I ate a lot of peanut butter and jelly sandwiches and spent too much time sleeping in my car or on the couches of people who seemed nice. I know it was a miracle I wasn't raped. I made enough money to get by, but nothing to send home. There wasn't enough work for a woman who wanted to sell the sight of her body as opposed to her body itself.

❊   ❊   ❊

Christmas card photograph taken by me of my mother and father sitting on the couch. Dad and Mom wear red sweatsuits and Santa hats. Dad eats a donut and looks off to one side while Mom sits on his lap and smiles too broadly.

By the time I came home in the beginning of October, I had my health, my leaking car, two shoeboxes full of pencils and postcards and pins I'd picked up along the way, and two nice clean holes in my hands. With the plugs in, the holes weren't that noticeable. If I'd only been worried about myself, I wouldn't have felt bad about returning with no money, but I was ashamed I hadn't managed to save anything for my parents. I'd prepared a lie for my mother about the holes being the result of some horrific funnel-cake grease accident, how I'd needed the money I saved to pay for the medical bills, but when she saw the holes she just sighed.

"At least you're home safe," she said. I guess she didn't have the energy to fret too much as there were other things to worry about. Dad was still living on the couch in the new trailer. Mom was working twelve hours a day to pay for the trailer and Dad's medical bills.

I got a waitressing job at a diner and moved in with a friend who was studying to be a dental hygienist.

"I should have a place of my own since I'm an adult," I told my mother.

"You could still stay with us," she said with a slight smile.

"It's kind of small," I said. She nodded. I think we both knew I didn't want to see my dad every day. Or smell him. Sunday dinner was difficult enough, with Mom trying to coax Dad to the table for twenty minutes before she gave up and ate cold pot roast with me.

"I think he's getting better," she told me every Sunday. There was nothing else to say.

I got a job at a doll factory when I got tired of the diner, of being on my feet, of truckers eyeing my ass, and of freaking them out when I took the pink plastic plug out of my left hand and poured their coffee refills through the hole in a careful, thin stream.

❧ ❧ ❧

Polaroid of funeral flowers sent by my father's sister in Akron. Arrangement consists of white roses and white lilies and white daisies, looks washed-out and spooky. My aunt wanted me to take a picture of the arrangement to send back to her so she could be sure the florist had done a good job, sent what she ordered, and not gone cheap on her.

Eighteen months after I ended my career as a human fountain and six months after I started working in the factory, my dad passed away. I don't know if there is a medical name for what happened to him, but somehow he moved backwards, lost coordination and bowel control and speaking skills, started drooling and had to wear diapers. He was fifty-three years old and helpless as an infant. The coroner said it was heart failure. It just stopped beating.

I took a week off work to help Mom out. She spent most of the time sitting at the kitchen table and unbending paperclips, making the wires into straight lines. I cooked for her, tidied the trailer, washed the floors, sponged the couch with vinegar and baking soda to rid it of the smell of my father, or, more exactly, the smell of his waste products. Mom didn't want me to, came and sat on the couch when she realized what I was doing. After that I cleaned around her. It seemed like the best way I could help.

I didn't know what to say to my mother, sometimes just sat beside her on the vinegar-and-baking-soda couch and slipped unbent paperclips through the metal tubes in my hands.

"Do you think you might want to move closer to me?" I asked her. Since I'd started working at the doll factory I'd gotten an apartment of my own. It was a bit noisy at times, but I liked it better than my parents' trailer. The brick building felt sturdier.

My mother watched me playing with her paperclips and shook her head. We'd both tried to help my father, to save him, and it hadn't worked. She kept working at her factory. I kept working at mine.

That's the way it's been for the past eight years.

※   ※   ※

Black-and-white photocopy picture of me tying a doll's hair back with a big gray bow. Picture is on the front of a booklet that is given to new employees at the factory about company policies and safety hazards. (The gray bow would be pink if they'd spent more for color copies.) In the picture I am smiling because my co-worker Gerry who took the photo has just told a raunchy joke.

The plastic dolls arrive in boxes, one hundred sixteen to the box. The pink dresses and green dresses and lavender dresses come in bags, fifty to a bag, assorted colors. The bows we tie ourselves out of quarter-inch ribbon. The paint for the dolls' eyes comes in two-ounce jars with a label that says the paint fumes have been shown to cause cancer in California. Apparently they don't cause cancer anywhere else.

Sometimes I work at the station where we dress the dolls and tie back their hair. Sometimes I work at the station where we tie little bows and glue them on the dresses, one on each puffy sleeve and one at the waist. There is nothing on the glue bottle about glue fumes causing cancer in any of the fifty states, but it smells like it probably does. Sometimes I work at the station where we paint the dolls' eyes blue and nails pink so the box can say hand-crafted.

No matter what station I'm at, sometimes in the middle of my shift I sit for a moment with a partially-finished doll in my hands and see that her fingers are curled in the same way my fingers want to curl at the end of a workday. The plastic that forms their bodies is not unlike the plastic plugs I use in my hands—rigid with a little give. After ten seconds of reflection, Judith the supervisor yells at me that this is not a tea party and I should get back to work.

By slowly increasing the size of the metal tubes in my hands over the past ten years, I've been able to enlarge the holes from a quarter-inch to three-quarters of an inch. The larger diameter means that more water could shoot through the holes.

"I don't understand why you want to make the holes bigger," my mother says.

"Because I can," I say. "Why have quarter-inch holes in your hands when you can have three-quarter-inch holes in your hands? It sounds more impressive." I don't tell her I haven't given up the idea of going back on the road.

❊   ❊   ❊

Photo #4 (from personal collection)—My living room/kitchen area. Posters of San Francisco and Chicago and New Orleans on the walls, blue secondhand couch under posters, twelve-inch television between couch and kitchen table so I can watch while eating. Two dolls, awards from work, sit on the television. They have blond hair and pink dresses with merit patches sewn on them because my boss is a cheapskate.

My mother drives over to my apartment for dinner once a week, brings bread and a vegetable, and I make some sort of main course. She still lives an hour away, alone in the same trailer she bought after the first one exploded.

"How is work?" she says right after she steps inside.

"Fine," I say, hugging her. "Did you go to that recipe swap meeting like you said you were going to?"

"Didn't have anything worth taking," she says. "Not in the mood for cooking, anyway. Gwen who lives next door to me, her daughter works at the auto plant, but you know she's going to school at night. Becoming an accountant."

"That's good," I say. "You really should try that recipe club again. Or maybe a garden club." She never seems really sad when I see her, but she never seemed really sad when my dad was going crazy. It's hard to know what I can believe.

146

"No space for flowers," she says. "You've got a head for numbers. Night school isn't that expensive. You could afford some classes."

"I'll think about it," I tell her. "I just worry about you getting lonely. You're not involved in anything social. When's the last time you went out for coffee with someone? Or on a date?"

"I'm fine," she sighs.

The first few minutes of every conversation are like this, trying to convert each other. I worry that my mother is lonely and depressed and turning into a hermit. My mother is upset because she hoped I wouldn't end up working in a factory like her and my father. She thinks I could have done something better than tying bows. Maybe designed the dolls or the dresses for the dolls or the boxes that the dolls are sold in or drawn an ad to market the dolls. She thinks what I'm doing is insignificant. Maybe she also thinks what she does is insignificant, but that doesn't seem to matter as much to her.

I don't mind the factory, and I don't figure that after a few thousand dollars and four years of college classes I'd find something I liked a lot more. Planning an advertising campaign to market the dolls doesn't seem more exciting to me than painting their eyes, and if I weren't painting their eyes, someone else would be.

Mom peers at the dolls on my television for the umpteenth time, shakes her head.

"I like the job," I tell her. "It's relaxing sometimes. Nice people work there. We chat."

"You chat," she says and cuts a wax bean into tiny pieces.

"What's wrong with chatting?" I say. "We're being social. We're helping the time pass."

She shrugs.

My mother worries that I am not special. Or at least less special that she would have liked. She doesn't see the holes as anything important. As me trying to help the family. But maybe that's just because it didn't work.

❆ ❆ ❆

Black-and-white picture of my father with his arms crossed, leaning against his Maverick (Mom says it was blue) and smirking. He wears jeans and a white t-shirt. The picture was taken shortly after my parents were married. The right corner is burnt and the whole image grayed with smoke.

My mother spends most of her free time restoring photos of my father, going over them again and again with a kneadable eraser, trying to get more of the soot off. She's arranged the pictures into new albums and has been writing down snatches of memory, what she recalls of my father, on index cards and sliding them into plastic sleeves beside the pictures. She brings out her albums after dinner, totes them over every week to show me her progress on the soot removal, though it's been ten years since the explosion and I don't think any more of the damage can be erased.

"I think they're looking better," she says. "Brighter."

"Sure," I say. "It's nice what you're doing."

※　※　※

Half of a black-and-white picture of my grandfather in a newsboy's gray cap and white shirt and dark pants. His palms are up, showing off the holes in his hands. The left side of the picture is black with char.

I don't think my mother knows that I have twenty photos of my grandfather, taken from the box of pictures under her bed. She never paid much attention to the pictures of Grandpa unless Dad was in them. Some of the photos are burned badly, damage beyond soot, but I've made copies of them and cut out the dark spaces, am trying to draw what was there before the fire. On the nights when I don't go out with the ladies from the factory, I'm at home working on the pictures of my grandfather, restoring his arms and legs. I know that he must have had wanderlust sometimes, moments when he still wanted to go out on the road.

I'm starting to map out a route, to find contacts along the way, more tattoo parlors and piercing studios that would sponsor me as a momentary celebrity. I have four thousand dollars saved up for the tour. A real one this time.

※　※　※

Photo #5 (from personal collection) — Picture of me and my mother. She holds one side of the camera with her left hand and I hold the other side with my right. Our faces are big and close together.

I try to smile like my father smiled. Wide. Uninhibited. The smile he had during those last few months when he was living on the brown corduroy couch and eating donuts. He looked happy like a six-year-old would look happy. He didn't want to be fifty-three any more. He wanted to be six a second time. Maybe he didn't think there was anything else for him to do. But what else was there for my mother to do but try and convince him to be fifty-three?

Now she leaves college brochures on the kitchen table while I'm in the bathroom, ones for me to find when she has left. I slip telephone numbers into her purse, widows who live in my apartment building and meet to play rummy on Thursdays. We do this and are both content for another week.

In the picture you cannot see the Band-Aids on her fingers. You cannot see the holes in mine.

Jen Hoppa, photograph

Pavane for a Summer Night

Forward and back in 4/4 time,
ladies and lords in Renaissance
courts danced in mannered,
preordained steps. But we

were in high school, off to summer
music camp in the hot middle
of California, University of the Pacific
at Stockton. Strangers gathered

for orchestra or Mr. Tomachefsky's
piano master class. Marty played
Charles Griffes' "Clouds," I played Satie,
Russell played Bach with his passionate

face right down at the keys. Laurie,
whose last name was French, played
Ravel's "Pavane for a Dead Princess."
That stately movement, the yearning,

and we were filled with it that summer,
lights out at 9 p.m. and the night just started,
yearning to dip our toes into the cool,
black night river. We snuck out
of the dorms, back door propped open

with a comb, to meet under an oak
in the wide grass. My feet were bare
as often as possible that year. I wanted
nothing between me and what there was
to feel. On this, we all agreed. In our cutoffs,
halter tops, and t-shirts, we needed to be out

in the night, touching the dark, touching
each other. We wandered the campus
by moonlight, speculating on the meaning

of Pavane. No sheet music, key signatures,
chord charts. Changing rhythms and modes,
we began to Pavane, and it was

roaming in the night without
supervision, rules or a plan, out
past curfew and locked doors.
We became Dukes and Duchesses
of the Pavanian Alps, and pavanes were

everything we wanted, still so far away,
over mountains and lakes, across oceans. Tom,
the trumpet player, held my hand as we ran

with Menno, who played upright bass, John
from Idaho, Russell who had a crush on Rose,
Michelle the flute player who smoked
so she wouldn't gain weight, and Laurie,
who spoke French and taught me
that rapturous first elided phrase —

like a song — *je suis heureuse* — such a small
group of sounds that propelled me,
four years later, to Paris. But for now

we followed the sounds of Ravel's
Pavane, high on the promise,
just out of reach, glistening

in our minds, like our skin
that night, every pore open.

from *The Rachel Nausicaa Suite*

Retrieving His Body

Like he was throwing a baseball.

Like he was reaching for a last ripe olive
to place in his 5-year-old's hand.

Nausicaa in blue does not dream.
She visions what the forest and insects will do.

We softstep out to retrieve his body.
Someone yells, "Internationals. Do not shoot."
The IDF shoots, close, then even closer.

Three thousand years a blood desert.

Privilege. In my gut. But they live
like this. Every day.

I can wash dishes. Can I carry my share?

Body outline: like he wanted to grab the bullet
that killed him.

*The Rachel Nausicaa Suite tells the story of Rachel Corrie, who grew up
in Olympia, Washington. When she was 23, she traveled to Palestine, and
worked there non-violently for peace and human rights. She was killed by a
bulldozer on March 16, 2003. Nausicaa is an allusion to the heroine, so committed to saving lives, in Hayao Miyazaki's *Nausicaa of the Valley of the Wind*.

Days by the River

for Joseph Strasko, Sr.

The owl sang
close to my window
the day after your death
and that night strong winds and gusts
of water fell hard against the doors.

I think you'd want to know this—
and that the river swelled
with a harsh rain.

The next day red clay ran with the current
and by nightfall all was peaceful.
The water matched the color
of sunset that evening.

You'd recognize
the orange-berried shrub
behind the house, the one
that keeps its green through winter
and you'd name it with your eyes.

Your sons don't want to mourn you
but they have your gifts.
They know the names of orchids,
of groundcovers, and their gardens lean toward
the sun. You offered me the steadiness

my own father tried to give me but
he left the earth too soon. You gave your
grandchildren your time as constant as the pines,
as holly, and the geese that never leave.

Today the river still runs
fast, and your echo runs with it.
I have missed so much already, I say,
and know you'd understand.

My Song

My ancestors sought their song in the purple of enemy blood
Dante sought his in the divine beauty of Beatrice
and Petrarch had Laura to spur him on

I seek mine in the overgrown cemeteries
of those who died fighting for our freedoms
I scour the un-weeded fields
and walk the abandoned pathways
where dreams struggle with weeds for a glimpse of light;
and in the solitude
I see seedlings of songs to be

I have seen patches of song peer
from the furrowed face of a blue-collar worker;
another lay slung over the bruised shoulder
of my enlisted brother.
I have had tunes carved out of the growls
of empty stomachs of exiled orphans.
With trembling fingers of the soul
I have touched many an enduring poem engraved
on the bones of those massacred in the name of peace. I have
picked cadence and rhythm, meter and metaphor
in the thud of boots crossing bridges to breach
the sanctity of man.
So do not ask where I get my song
nor why it must come forth in such hoarse voice.

The day has ravens in it

Out on the road on the lip
of the tar, perched on the fence
by the compost bin, in the nextdoor yard:
with bold glass eye and satin coat
sleek with black all the way
down to ash, three of them
survey and own. They own all of it

today. And when the air throws its wings
wide along tunnels of world
fleeing wind's flail,
as solid in tone
as the singular night of belly and breast,
the plumage like shoes shone, a track's rediscovered
at a tearing. It's Friday

again; the rend
exposes shames long lived through but fresh as the itch
in throat and eye. There's chalk
in the fingers of the wind. Nails
scratch on soul: rough diamond on long-playing
record, the vinyl slightly
warped. Forgiveness—

impossible as it seems in this roar
of world—also lights on the gray suburban
fence, eye fixed on things that might
sustain or shelter, voice a
rasp that levels and draws
a family with it, down tracks
forgotten, inevitable, and

fresh.

Another Complaint

When they cut down the dogwood
in our yard, we dismembered
the trunk and branches with hand-
saws, stacked and twined the limbs,
snapped the twigs and finer gray
tendrils in our raw small hands,
collapsing buds in bunches
and bagging them in plastic
left on the side of the road.

The stump remained an empty
plinth for weeks, as Christmas came
and evenings crept up the lawn.
My sister was done with school
(where my mother never went,
where my father never went)
where she majored in Fine Art
& Literature: now she took
the train into the city
to work as the assistant
to an editor of "soft-
core pornography," they liked
to joke about their only
daughter, when it was romance
literature really. I'd found
a poem she'd written that fall
of a girl who kept sliding
down into the infernal
bowels of the New York City
sewer like she was nothing
more than a scrap of paper.
In a few months my father
would kick her out, for crying
all the time. But for Christmas

they exhumed her art thesis
from the basement: a soldered

bird of some kind — an eagle
or phoenix maybe, something
mythic and secret and bad
and also somehow funny
for how close it came to art:
shard-beaked, serrated feathers,
talons reptilian with wings
outstretched and flexed in gruesome,
frustrated flight. For reasons

no one could comprehend then
our father and our mother
bolted that bird to our tree
stump, facing the street, festooned
its iron wings with colored
lights, then left her there burning
well into the wet new year.

Francisco Toledo, drypoint

Against Restraint

for Delaney, b. 9/7/08

Next door, the blackout shades are drawn
by seven, as if nothing were left to be seen,
neither lowering sky nor wind in the poplars.

Even now, as you are shaking slowly free
of another body, the stoops and balconies stand empty,
the windows shuttered, the cars garaged.

What little breeze moves through yards
of regimented flowers and grassblades seems to say:
Come, be reasonable. Want less.

Somewhere in the neighborhood, someone burned
yard clippings all afternoon. Now sundown
sets the sky and empty streets alight

and a low fog of smoke drifts blue-white
among the trees like passion, like mercy.
If I ask you how many skies

before you no longer wish to see sky,
promise me your answer will always be
No number great enough.

Green Ghazal

A new century rolls over the prime meridian on a hill in Greenwich
the way two dogs tumble beyond their master's reach across the green.

Christmas came and went and we did not sing Mele Kalikimaka with Bing;
the frost-scorched world disfigured the new year, bleached out the evergreens.

Watch as I turn myself to a blond Frenchwoman with the kitchen's alchemy;
watch as I flee, without running, my childhood's dry meat and boiled greens.

Autumn's raku pots are tonged from the kiln and buried in trash cans of dry leaves,
the molten glass on their shoulders choking as it burns into copper, pitted green.

In January, my mother hears uilleann pipes, bodhran. *Erinn*, she says, I *named you
for an island*, and I see how she sees me: foundering at sea, a doomed speck of green.

From the collection of the Editor, photograph

Words at Play: Dark Matter and Sticky Stuff

My topic this evening is "Words at Play." My subtitle is "Dark Matter & Sticky Stuff." If the phrases "dark matter" and "sticky stuff" sound as if they refer to things I can't see and things I can't shake, you have it right. I borrowed them from astronomy and quantum physics.

I like ideas to have a little dirt on their shoes. Therefore, I was not just delighted but downright giddy when the astronomers came up with the term "dark matter" to refer to what they *can't* see that lies between what they *can* see. In other words, "dark matter" is the stuff *between* the stuff. Meanwhile, the quantum physicists decided to refer to what holds together the smallest recordable elements of the atom as . . . what else? "sticky stuff." How better to refer to what we can't see and can't escape? I may not be able to follow Einstein's theory of relativity, but I feel I understand in my bones the concepts of "dark matter" and "sticky stuff." I have not traveled in outer space, I do not leave my body, I have never—not even once—been abducted by aliens, I am not in touch with spirits from the past, I am neither a psychic nor a seer, but I have been living with dark matter and sticky stuff my whole life.

Think about it. Writing is about . . . dark matter and sticky stuff. So are philosophy and religion. Morality, ethics and anything sociopolitical are about dark matter and sticky stuff.

How, then, in a universe of dark matter and sticky stuff, can we encourage—indeed, even validate—an idea of writing as "words at play"? Well, writers to whom the very language matters—which is to say, any writer one would wish to reread—such writers do not so much express in their work what they knew beforehand as what they didn't know they knew. When you think about it, that's not so strange. We all do this in conversation, confidently dogpaddling forward without quite knowing where we will end up. To anyone who insists that we "get to the point," or "cut to the chase," we might respond, as a frustrated writing student said to the novelist E. M. Forster, "How do I know what I mean till I see what I say?"

---

*Marvin Bell presented this keynote address at the 31st *Nimrod* Awards Presentation on October 23rd, 2009. Copyright Marvin Bell, 2010.

There is a fair amount of improvisation in the arts, a good deal of flying by the seat of one's pants and going on one's nerve, lots of accident and a whole lot of dumb luck. Now I believe wholeheartedly in dumb luck. But you have to make yourself available to it. Hence, artists accumulate techniques, but they also trust their instincts. It's hard to get writers, in particular, to 'fess up about how they make art because they fear that, if they tell you the truth, you won't respect them in the morning.

Nor is it always possible to explain. The story goes that one of George Balanchine's dancers asked him what the ballet they were rehearsing was about. In order to dance it, she said, she needed to know the story. But Balanchine wasn't one of those choreographers who thought ballets needed to tell a story, and he said, "It's not about *anything*; it's just steps." But the dancer said again that she simply had to know what the ballet was about, and Balanchine said, "Okay, then, it's about *time*." And the dancer said, "What do you mean it's about time?" And Balanchine said, "It's about fifteen minutes long."

There is a quatrain by the Spanish poet, Antonio Machado, just four lines of poetry, that speaks to this matter of not knowing ahead of time:

People possess four things
that are no good at sea:
anchor, rudder, oars
and the fear of going down.

Well, I grew up on the Atlantic Ocean, and, like many of you I know the importance of an anchor, a rudder, a set of oars, and even a healthy fear of drowning to remind one to play it safe. So what's the point? The point is, why go to the same islands all the time? Why encourage the same outcome every time? Why not abandon oneself to the medium, to the materials, and end up somewhere previously unrealized? Why not try what the poet William Stafford liked to call "adventuring in the language"? Maybe imaginative writing, written freely, will find, once in a while, new expressions of the human condition. For imaginative writing, just as much as wordless music, is finally about our inner lives. It is about what life feels like.

When it comes to what life feels like, words often fail us, and at other times none are needed. But what if sometimes we need to find the words that express more than the material moment? Raw emotion by itself won't do. When we hear a person screaming, we usually can't tell what he or she is saying.

Nor does yelling say much more than "ouch!" Imagine, for a moment, that I latch onto one of you later tonight, and I grab you by your lapels and I say, "Listen, I have to tell you something. Whatever good and beautiful feelings and thoughts we contain — love, faith, charity, compassion — we also sometimes contain not so good and not so beautiful thoughts and feelings. Even hate." And I could try to convince you by pulling you close and staring into your eyes like Robert Mitchum playing the part of an itinerant preacher in the movie *The Night of the Hunter*, in which he has L-O-V-E written on the knuckles of one hand and H-A-T-E on the knuckles of the other — I could pull you close and chant, "Hate! Hate! Hate!"

And what would be the effect of that? Well, for one thing, you might mistake me for Glenn Beck, and you'd want to get away. But suppose I said it this way:

My Hate

My hate is like ripe fruit
from an orchard, which is mine.

I sink my teeth into it.
I nurse on its odd shapes.

I have grafted every new variety,
walked in my bare feet,

rotting and detached,
on the fallen ones.

Vicious circle. Unfriendly act.
I am eating the whole world.

In the caves of my ill will
I must be stopped.

That, I think, has a different effect. Some years ago, in a high school in Chicago, a student told me she had seen that poem and was afraid of me, and I had to reassure her I wasn't like that.

So much for trying to pin down hate. Let's take up love. I should tell you that last summer my wife and I made love on the sidewalk. A young woman in Port Townsend, Washington, had arranged quarters on the concrete to nearly spell out, in big letters, "L-O-V-E." There were still a few spaces among the letters, so when she asked us if we wanted to "make love on the sidewalk," she got our attention.

The young panhandler had turned an abstraction into something tangible. The trouble with abstractions like love and hate is that by themselves they have no specific meanings. No one knows what "I love you" means. We each have to fill in the meaning from our experience. Poetry and its cousin, song, are often used simply to try to say, "I love you."

Now, I tend to write poetry only when the pot boils over, though of course over the years I have learned how to turn up the heat. But one day, without waiting for the temperature to rise, I set out to write a love poem for my wife, Dorothy. Christmas was coming. If I could write one in time, I could have it secretly printed and framed and wrap it in a big box for Christmas.

The trouble with trying to write a love poem is that everyone knows what a love poem says. The world is chockablock with love poems. Thus, I would have to find a surprising line with which to begin, a line I could play with. I called my poem "To Dorothy," and this is how I began it: "You are not beautiful, exactly." Well, if you write that line to your wife, you had damn well better write a second line. This is the poem, which is called, simply, "To Dorothy."

To Dorothy

You are not beautiful, exactly.
You are beautiful, inexactly.
You let a weed grow by the mulberry
and a mulberry grow by the house.
So close, in the personal quiet
of a windy night, it brushes the wall
and sweeps away the day till we sleep.

A child said it, and it seemed true:
"Things that are lost are all equal."
But it isn't true. If I lost you,
the air wouldn't move, nor the tree grow.
Someone would pull the weed, my flower.
The quiet wouldn't be yours. If I lost you,
I'd have to ask the grass to let me sleep.

Recently, I had occasion to search the Internet for a line from the middle of my poem "To Dorothy." I had suddenly wondered, after all these years, if I might have echoed someone else's line when I wrote, "Things that are lost are all equal." Sure enough, Google offered me hundreds of links. But they were all *me*. So then I ran an advanced search, first for the one line in question, and then for the first two lines of the poem, which are better known, this time ruling out my name, and still each time there were pages and pages of links. Some were my poem, in text fair or foul, with or without a byline, but many instances were other people's writing in which they had used my lines in their own pieces as if the words were their own. Of the few I looked at, the two I remember best were, first, a website with a handsome masthead proclaiming the title of the website, which is, "You are not beautiful, exactly. You are beautiful, inexactly..." and, second, a message board on which a woman was asking other women where on her body she should tattoo those two lines, since she intended to lose weight.

You might wonder if I was offended. Not at all. On the one hand, it's poetry! On the other hand, it's just poetry.

The quantum physicists tell us that the presence of an observer changes the results of the experiment. It is the same with words. In language, there is always slippage, from inaccuracy, from idiomatic distortion, from personal and cultural bias, and from scientific and social change. My language and yours are not identical. But our meanings overlap. If you say, "I'm about to punch you," I'll probably duck. As Henry David Thoreau put it, "Some evidence is incontrovertible, as for example when you find a trout in the milk."

Theorists of language often work in the areas where language does *not* overlap, pointing this out. Most writers work in the overlaps, though not always. When writers write in ways that are odd, unsettling or obscure, it is because they are trying to express something for which there are, in a sense, "no words," to get beyond language, to express the feeling *with* the words. The oddness, the eccentricity, the recklessness at times of imaginative writing, are not meant to conceal, but to reveal. Meanwhile, good writing listens to itself as it goes. Good writing is, in that sense, "words at play."

If there is always an element of play in good writing, why, in this difficult world, does playful writing matter? Wittgenstein said, "The limits of my language mean the limits of my world." And creative writing enlarges the world. More important, poetry and artful prose, like music, dance, painting, drama, and the plastic arts, express our soul. Indeed, I would wager that Americans approve of good literature far more than one can tell by book sales, or by how much is read outside the classroom. I think most people know that a nation's soul is expressed in its art.

And art is all about the imagination. Today, more than ever, in this age of the Internet and of 24/7 breaking news, when the human condition is constantly being thrust, as they say, "in our face," philosophy and the imagination are not luxuries. They are not just personal pleasures or college electives. They are survival skills, and we ignore them at our peril.

The poet Jack Gilbert imagined the place of writing in society in a poem which he titled, with his tongue in his cheek, "In Dispraise of Poetry."

In Dispraise of Poetry

When the King of Siam disliked a courtier,
He gave him a beautiful white elephant.
The miracle beast deserved such ritual
That to care for him properly meant ruin.
Yet to care for him improperly was worse.
It appears the gift could not be refused.

In the end, writers are people who are helpless *not* to write. And however serious the content of their writing, there is always the element of words at play.

My own poetry has increasingly referred to the news, to wartime and government, to the misuse and mistreatment of soldiers and veterans and to the hubris of empire. Nonetheless, for all the insistent socio-political issues we cannot escape, it is still true that most young writers, having begun to write for whatever reason, continue because they can't help it. Sometimes it's just the materials that have taken hold of them for what then turns into a lifetime. One of us loves rhythm and sound, another loves stories and character, a third adores syntax, a fourth is passionate for imagery, and a fifth is mad for metaphor. Or maybe we just like the way it feels to write. We all know many writers who rush to their desks to write so as not to have to do something else.

Now I want to say something about the character of writing classes and conferences. I think the most important characteristic of a good workshop is the sense that we are all in this together, students and teacher. Let me tell you a story. It's the '60s or early '70s. The crowd that has shown up to hear Allen Ginsberg is far too large for the room. Hundreds of people can't even get in the door. From the street, we pass the word forward that we are moving to a larger hall. Soon six or seven hundred people are following our little advance group across a greensward when a young man pushes forward to ask Ginsberg a question. "Whaddya think of Creeley's new book?" he asks. That's the poet, Robert Creeley. By the young man's tone of voice, we can tell that he himself doesn't think much of it. Another disappointed fan. But Ginsberg delivers a terrific response. Turning to the young man, he says, "Whatever Bob's doing, I'm *for* him." We could use a lot more of that.

If I may quote an old poem of mine: "We all know how many times a critic reads a book: less than once."

Well, it's a new world, this viral Internet world, which is redefining intellectual property rights and the business model for art. The community is rapidly abrogating the status of the individual. We need to remember that writing is, first of all, a way of life, not a career. The profession, the audience, the money that prose can earn, the fellowships and honors—such things are bonuses. And if you are in it, the reading and writing life, not for a career, but as a way of life, you are, as my father used to say, "cookin' with gas," and you are on the money, and you are, like Jack Kerouac's subterraneans, "hip but not slick, cool but not corny."

I thank you for your interest and your attention. I'll end with a poem called "White Clover." White clover pops up on our lawn in Iowa because the neighborhood was once farmland, and the clover was feed.

White Clover

Once when the moon was out about three-quarters
and the fireflies who are the stars
of backyards
were out about three-quarters
and about three-fourths of all the lights
in the neighborhood
were on because people can be at home,
I took a not so innocent walk
out among the lawns,
navigating by the light of lights,
and there there were many hundreds of moons
on the lawns
where before there was only polite grass.
These were moons on long stems,
their long stems giving their greenness
to the center of each flower
and the light giving its whiteness to the tops
of the petals. I could say
it was light from stars
touched the tops of flowers and no doubt
something heavenly reaches what grows outdoors
and the heads of men who go hatless,
but I like to think we have a world
right here, and a life
that isn't death. So I don't say it's better
to be right here. I say this is where
many hundreds of core-green moons
gigantic to my eye
rose because men and women had sown green grass,
and flowered to my eye in man-made light,
and to some would be as fire in the body
and to others a light in the mind
over all their property.

MICHAEL ANDREWS, co-founder/publisher/editor with Jack Grapes of Bombshelter Press and *ONTHEBUS*, is living, for the moment, in Hermosa Beach, California. He has published over ten books of poetry, twenty fine print poetry/photography portfolios, and a number of fine print pamphlets, murals, and broadsides, as well as photographic art prints.

LAUREL BASTIAN has work in *Margie*, *The Cream City Review*, and other journals, lives in Madison, Wisconsin, and attends the M.F.A. program there.

ERINN BATYKEFER is the author of *Allegheny, Monongahela* (Red Hen Press 2009), winner of the Benjamin Saltman Poetry Prize. Her poetry and prose have appeared recently in such journals as *Prairie Schooner*, *Sou'wester*, and *FIELD*. She is currently at work on a second collection and a memoir.

MARVIN BELL is the author of twenty books of poetry, including *Mars Being Red*, *Rampant*, *Nightworks: Poems 1962-2000*, *The Book of the Dead Man*, and *Stars Which See, Stars Which Do Not See*, a finalist for the National Book Award. His honors include awards from the American Academy of Arts and Letters, the Academy of American Poets, and *The American Poetry Review*. He taught for The University of Iowa Writers' Workshop for forty years, served two terms as Iowa's Poet Laureate, and now teaches for the brief-residency M.F.A. located in Oregon at Pacific University.

HELEN DEGEN COHEN's awards include the NEA (poetry), First Prize in British *Stand Magazine*'s fiction competition, and three Illinois Arts Council awards. She co-edits *RHINO* and was twice featured in *Spoon River*. 2009 publications include two collections—*Habry* and *On A Good Day One Discovers Another Poet*—plus a novel excerpt. She emigrated from Europe at twelve.

DANICA COLIC's poems have appeared in *Arts & Letters*, *RealPoetik*, *Pebble Lake Review*, and *Terrain*, and her chapbook is forthcoming from Love Among the Ruins. She resides in Brooklyn, where she curates Uncalled-For Readings.

NICOLE DiCELLO's work has appeared in publications such as *Poetry East*, *Mid-America Poetry Review*, and *Concho River Review*. Her manuscript *Redshift* was a finalist for the 2008 Bordighera Poetry Prize and is currently being circulated to publishers. She lives in Leominster, Massachusetts.

DEBORAH DIEMONT is a freelance writer living in Syracuse, New York. Her poems and poetry translations have recently appeared in *CAIRN, The*

Oleander Review, Lucid Rhythms, and *Stone Canoe*. She spends summers in San Cristóbal de las Casas, Chiapas, Mexico, where she translates video scripts and exhibit materials at the Museum of Mayan Medicine.

DANIEL DONAGHY's newest collection of poems, *Start with the Trouble*, was published by the University of Arkansas Press. His first collection, *Street-fighting*, was published by BkMk Press in 2005 and named a Finalist for the 2006 Paterson Poetry Prize.

EMIL DRAITSER is an award-winning author and a professor of Russian at Hunter College in New York City. He has published essays and short stories in the *Los Angeles Times, Partisan Review, North American Review, Prism International*, and many other American and Canadian periodicals. His fiction has also appeared in Russian, Polish, Ukrainian, Byelorussian, and Israeli journals. His most recent book is *Shush! Growing Up Jewish Under Stalin: A Memoir.*

SIMON PETER EGGERTSEN was born in Kansas, raised in Utah, and schooled in Virginia and England. His poems have been or will be published in *Dialogue, The Salt River Review, Lunarosity, Wordbridge, The Writers Post*, and *Istanbul Literary Review*. He won First Prize for Poetry at the Whidbey Island (Washington) Writers Conference, 2008.

ANNE ELVEY is a researcher and poet. She is the author of *An Ecological Feminist Reading of the Gospel of Luke: A Gestational Paradigm*. Her poems have appeared in journals including *Antipodes, Cordite, Eureka Street, Eremos, Meanjin* and *PAN*. In 2008, her work placed first in the *page seventeen* poetry competition and was highly commended in the Max Harris Poetry Award Competition.

TARFIA FAIZULLAH is a third-year poetry student in Virginia Commonwealth University's M.F.A. program. She is a 2007-08 AWP Intro Journals Award Winner. Her work has been published or is forthcoming in *Mid-American Review, Green Mountains Review, Ploughshares, Cimarron Review, The Southern Review*, and elsewhere.

LINDA RUI FENG was born in Shanghai and recently graduated from Columbia University with a Ph.D. in Chinese literature. She is currently living in Stillwater, Oklahoma, where she is working on a group of short stories.

KENNETH FROST's poems have appeared in *Bitter Oleander, Notre Dame Review, Confrontation, Southwest Review, Denver Quarterly*, and many other journals. He lives in Maine.

169

ROBERT GRUNST's work has been published in *American Literary Review*, *Crab Orchard Review*, *The Iowa Review*, *Seneca Review*, *The Saint Ann's Review*, and *Third Coast*. *The Smallest Bird in North America*, his first book, was published in 2000. A former Great Lakes gillnet fisherman, he is currently the chair of the English Department at The College of St. Catherine. "Bronzy Incas" is from a manuscript entitled *The Wreck of the Twilight*.

JACQUELINE GUIDRY's stories have appeared in *Louisiana Literature*, *Rosebud*, *Yemassee*, and other magazines. Her novel, *The Year the Colored Sisters Came to Town*, was selected as the 2003 United We Read book in Kansas City, Missouri, and the 2007 community read in Windsor, Connecticut. The story in this issue of *Nimrod* is from a collection which she is currently working on.

GEORGE HIGGINS is a public defender in Oakland, California. His poems have appeared or will soon appear in *Best American Poetry 2003*, *Pleiades*, *88*, *Poetry Flash*, *Southern Humanities Review*, and *The George Washington Review*, among other journals.

JANET JENNINGS lives in San Anselmo, California, with her husband and daughters. For twenty years she owned and ran Sunspire, a natural candy manufacturing company. Her poetry has appeared or is forthcoming in *Agni online*, *Atlantic Review*, *Bitter Oleander*, *Bryant Literary Review*, *California Quarterly (CQ)*, *Connecticut Review*, and *Poet Lore*, among other journals.

LACY M. JOHNSON recently earned a Ph.D. from The University of Houston's Creative Writing Program. Her creative and critical work has appeared or is forthcoming in *Memoir (and)*, *Gulf Coast*, *Irish Studies Review*, and *Pebble Lake Review*.

P M F JOHNSON's poems have previously appeared in *Nimrod*, *The Threepenny Review*, *Atlanta Review*, *The New York Quarterly*, *Blue Unicorn*, and other journals. Some of his haiku have been selected for reprinting in year's-best anthologies by The Red Moon Press.

HOLLY KARAPETKOVA's poems and translations from the Bulgarian have appeared in a number of journals and anthologies, including *Crab Orchard Review*, *The Marlboro Review*, *The Cream City Review*, *150 Contemporary Sonnets*, and the *International Poetry Anthology* (Slovenia). She teaches at Marymount University in the Washington, DC, area.

BECKY KENNEDY is a linguist and college professor and lives in Jamaica Plain, Massachusetts. Her publications include articles in theoretical and applied linguistics; her poetry has appeared in a number of magazines.

LANCE LARSEN's third collection of poems was published in 2008 by University of Tampa Press. Recent work has appeared or is forthcoming in *River Styx, Raritan, The Gettysburg Review, The Iowa Review, Black Warrior Review, The Georgia Review,* and elsewhere. His awards include a Pushcart Prize and fellowships from Sewanee, the Ragdale Foundation, and the National Endowment for the Arts. He teaches at Brigham Young University, where he serves as poetry editor of *Literature and Belief.*

MICHAEL LEVAN recently graduated with his M.F.A. in poetry from Western Michigan University, where he served as poetry editor of *Third Coast* and was an intern at New Issues Press. In Fall 2008, he will begin in the Ph.D. program at the University of Tennessee Knoxville.

DAVID LEWITZKY is a retired social worker/family therapist living in Buffalo, New York. His recent work has appeared in *River Oak Review, Red Wheelbarrow,* and *Nexus,* among other periodicals. "Kazatzke" is one section of a book-length work in progress titled *Dream Of Myself As The Non-Stop Dancing Master.*

ROY MASH is an electronics technician living in Marin County, California. His work has been published or is forthcoming in *Atlanta Review, RHINO, The Evansville Review, Poetry Midwest, Two Review, miller's pond,* and several *Marin Poetry Center Anthologies.* He was Second Prize winner in the 2008 *Two Review* Poetry Contest judged by Marvin Bell.

BRYAN D. METS is currently a graduate student working towards a dual doctorate in Biochemistry and Molecular Biology and Environmental and Integrative Toxicological Sciences at Michigan State University. He lives in Lansing with a kitten, a banjo, and a roommate. The situation is not quite as humorous as one might hope.

TERESA MILBRODT received her M.F.A. in creative writing from Bowling Green State University. Her stories have appeared in *North American Review, Crazyhorse, The Cream City Review, Hayden's Ferry Review, Sycamore Review,* and *Passages North,* among other literary magazines. Her work has also been nominated for a Pushcart Prize. She teaches creative writing at Western State College of Colorado.

JESSICA MOLL was born and raised in the San Francisco Bay Area, where she now makes her home. She received a B.A. from University of California, Berkeley, and an M.F.A. in creative writing from Eastern Washington University. Her work has appeared or is forthcoming in *Knockout, RHINO,* and *Hiram Poetry Review.*

KEITH MONTESANO's first book, *Ghost Lights*, a finalist for the 2008 Orphic Prize, will be published by Dream Horse Press in 2010. Other poems have appeared or are forthcoming in *Hayden's Ferry Review*, *American Literary Review*, *Third Coast*, *Ninth Letter*, *Crab Orchard Review*, *Another Chicago Magazine*, *River Styx*, *Hunger Mountain*, and elsewhere. He is currently a Ph.D. Candidate in English at Binghamton University.

PETER MUNRO is a fisheries scientist who works in the Bering Sea, the Aleutian Islands, the Gulf of Alaska, and Seattle.

CLEMENT NDULUTE is an Associate Professor of English at Tuskegee University in Alabama. He has published many articles of criticism on African poetry and African American literary connections with Africa. Two of his books are *Shujaa Okonkwo*, a Swahili translation of Chinua Achebe's novel *Things Fall Apart*, and *The Poetry of Shaaban Robert*, a selection of poetry by this renowned author, with a critical introduction.

ADELE NE JAME has lived in Hawaii since 1969. She has published two books of poems and is completing a third, *Sea Flight*. Among many prizes, she has received a National Endowment for the Arts award in poetry. She has taught poetry at the University of Hawaii-Manoa, served as Poet-in-Residence at the University of Wisconsin-Madison, and is currently teaching poetry at Hawaii Pacific University.

SUSAN DWORSKI NUSBAUM is a retired criminal prosecutor living in Buffalo, New York. She has been a frequent participant in the Chautauqua Institution Writers' Festival and poetry workshops, where her poems have won several prizes. Her work has appeared or is awaiting publication in *Connecticut Review*, *Chautauqua Literary Journal*, *Harpur Palate*, *Artvoice*, and *The Buffalo News*.

KARA OAKLEAF is an M.F.A. student at George Mason University where she also works for the Association of Writers and Writing Programs. She lives in Alexandria, Virginia, and is currently working on a novel.

ANDREA O'BRIEN's poetry has appeared or is forthcoming in various publications, including *The Hopkins Review*, *Connecticut Review*, *North American Review*, and *The New York Quarterly*. In 2007, the Kentucky Foundation for Women awarded her an Artist Enrichment grant to begin writing her second collection of poems. She lives in central Kentucky with her husband and works as a freelance writer and editor.

DAN O'BRIEN's work has appeared or is forthcoming in *Greensboro Review*, *The Pinch*, *Crab Orchard Review*, *Alaska Quarterly Review*, *South Carolina*

Review, and elsewhere. He was the 2006-07 Hodder Fellow playwright-in-residence at Princeton University, and he recently spent three semesters as the Tennessee Williams Fellow at Sewanee, The University of the South. Upcoming play productions include *The Cherry Sisters Revisited* at the 2010 Humana Festival of New American Plays at Actor's Theatre of Louisville.

JUDITH TATE O'BRIEN's collection, *Mythic Places*, won the ByLine Press 2000 Chapbook contest and the Oklahoma Book Award. *By the Grace of Ghosts*, a collection co-written with poet Jane Taylor and published in 2003, was a finalist in the Oklahoma Center for the Book Award, as was *Everything That Is, Is Connected* published in 2005. Her poems have been published in journals including *Calyx*, *Poet Lore*, and *Hubbub*.

MICHAEL LEE PHILLIPS, a graduate of Fresno State University, lives and writes in the high desert of Southern California, after residing for a time in Greece and Ireland. He has work forthcoming in *Beloit Poetry Journal*, *Pearl*, *The New York Quarterly*, and *Stinging Fly* (Ireland).

ANDREA POTOS is the author of the poetry collections *Yaya's Cloth* (Iris Press) and *The Perfect Day* (Parallel Press). Her poems appear widely in journals and anthologies.

LINDA RAMEY is the winner of the Rhode Island State Arts Council Fellowship in Literature. She holds an M.F.A. in creative writing from the University of Maryland. Her work has appeared in *New Letters*, *Onearth*, *Nimrod*, *The MacGuffin*, *The Rocky Mountain Review*, *Salamander*, *Prairie Schooner*, and other publications. She teaches English at the Community College of Rhode Island in Newport, Rhode Island.

OLIVER RICE has received the Theodore Roethke Prize and has twice been nominated for a Pushcart Prize. His poems have appeared widely in journals and anthologies in the U.S., as well as in Canada, England, Austria, Turkey, and India. His book of poems, *On Consenting to Be a Man*, has been introduced by Cyberwit, a diversified publishing house in the cultural capital Allahabad, India.

LEE ROSSI's most recent book is *Ghost Diary* (Terrapin Press, 2003). His poetry, reviews, and interviews have appeared widely in such journals as *The Sun*, *Poetry East*, *Chelsea*, *Green Mountains Review*, *The Spoon River Poetry Review*, and *Beloit Poetry Journal*. A staff reviewer and interviewer for the online magazine *Pedestal*, he lives in the San Francisco Bay Area.

MICHELE RUBY acts, tap-dances, and writes in Louisville, Kentucky, where she teaches fiction writing at Bellarmine University. Her stories appear in *The Louisville Review, Lilith, Rosebud, The Adirondack Review* (Fulton Prize finalist), *Denver Quarterly, The MacGuffin,* and several other journals. She has an M.F.A. in fiction from Spalding University.

F. DANIEL RZICZNEK's books include *Divination Machine* (just released in 2009), *Neck of the World,* and *Cloud Tablets.* He is coeditor, with Gary L. McDowell, of *The Rose Metal Press Field Guide to Prose Poetry: Contemporary Poets in Discussion and Practice,* forthcoming in 2010. He has published poems in numerous literary venues nationwide and currently teaches English composition at Bowling Green State University.

LAUREN SCHMIDT's work may be found or is forthcoming in *Audemus, Slab,* and *Ruminate,* where her poem, "The Unseasoned Earth," was a finalist for the 2008 Janet B. McCabe Poetry Prize. A New Jersey native, she lives and teaches high school English and art history in Eugene, Oregon.

LYNN SHOEMAKER grew up beside the Missouri River. He has done much peace marching and human rights traveling. He has written poetry for nearly 50 years, and his most recent book is *Hands.*

GEORGE SINGER is a professor of special education at the University of California, Santa Barbara. His poems have appeared in *Prairie Schooner, Tar River Poetry, Nimrod,* and other journals. He is a former Zen Buddhist monk and priest and he tries to write poetry informed by this experience.

BARBARA BUCKMAN STRASKO is the first Poet Laureate of Lancaster County. She is honored to be named the 2009 Teacher of the Year by River of Words, an environmental art and poetry program for children. Her poems have appeared in: *The Best New Poets of 2006, RHINO, Spoon River Poetry Review, Tar River Review, Brilliant Corners,* and *Ninth Letter.* Her chapbook *On the Edge of a Delicate Day* was published by Pudding House Press in 2008.

KATE SWEENEY's work has appeared or is forthcoming in *Poetry East, Meridian, New Orleans Review, RATTLE,* and *Tampa Review.* Her chapbook, *Better Accidents,* is forthcoming from YellowJacket Press. She currently lives in Tampa and teaches English.

RICHARD TENEYCK is a retired English teacher, who has published poetry in various journals and has been nominated for a Pushcart Prize and takes much of his inspiration from the geography of the Lake Ontario orchard country in western New York State, where he has always lived.

CAROL WAS is the poetry editor of *The MacGuffin* at Schoolcraft College. In addition to *Nimrod*, her poems have appeared or are forthcoming in *Connecticut Review*, *Margie*, *Sycamore Review*, *The Gettysburg Review*, and *Isotope*, and have been read on Martha Stewart Living Radio. She is an active member of Springfed Arts—Metro Detroit Writers.

A. E. WATKINS currently attends Purdue University's Graduate English Program and is a graduate of the M.F.A. program at Saint Mary's College of California. His poetry can be found in or is forthcoming from *Dislocate Magazine*, *American Poetry Journal*, *Copper Nickel*, and *Barrow Street*.

DEDE WILSON is the author of three books of poems: *Glass*, *Sea of Small Fears*, and *One Nightstand*. Her poetry has appeared in journals including *The Carolina Quarterly*, *The Spoon River Poetry Review*, *Poem*, *The Cream City Review*, and *Tar River Poetry*. She has also published short stories and a memoir, *Fourth Child, Second Daughter*. A full-length manuscript, *Eliza: The New Orleans Years*, has been a finalist in the Perugia Press Competition and the Pearl Poetry Prize.

WILLIAM KELLEY WOOLFITT's poems in this issue are from his completed book-length sequence, *Words for Flesh: a Spiritual Autobiography of Charles de Foucauld*. He teaches writing at Pennsylvania State University and works as a backpacking guide at a summer camp in New Hampshire. His poems and short stories have been published or are forthcoming in *The Spoon River Poetry Review*, *Shenandoah*, *Poetry International*, *North Dakota Quarterly*, *Weber Studies*, *Sycamore Review*, *The Cincinnati Review*, and *Nimrod*, among other journals.

CAROL BIERER is a graphic artist, painter, and poet.

GERALD COURNOYER is a member of the Oglala Sioux tribe from Marty, South Dakota. He received an M.F.A. in Painting from the University of Oklahoma. He has exhibited work in group and solo exhibitions, including several solo shows in New Mexico, South Dakota, Texas, Oklahoma, and Shanghai, China. He is represented in Tulsa by M. A. Doran Gallery.

OTTO DUECKER has been exploring Realism for over thirty years. His work has been exhibited in New York, Illinois, California, New Mexico, and Oklahoma, and is featured in many collections. He graduated from Oklahoma State University. He is represented in Tulsa by M. A. Doran Gallery.

JEN HOPPA graduated from The University of Tulsa. She is a photographer who has taught photography and humanities classes at local colleges.

MANLY JOHNSON is a poet, teacher, and visual artist. He was *Nimrod*'s poetry editor for many years. His latest volume of poems is *Holding on to What Is: New & Selected Poems*.

SAM JOYNER's work has been selected for numerous exhibitions, receiving various awards, including First Place Best of Show at the 1995 Lawton Arts Festival and juror's awards in the 1998 and 1999 Tulsa International Mayfest. He is the Chair of the *Nimrod* Advisory Board.

ZAC KING was a student at Edison High School in Tulsa. The photograph in this issue was part of the Telling My Story Project, funded by the Kennedy Center for the Arts.

LARISA LEONOVA lives in Novosibirsk, Siberia where she has been an English teacher, psychologist, art director, poet, and photographer. She describes herself as curious, intuitive, and always ready for change.

NATHAN OPP is a painter whose work has been exhibited in numerous galleries and museums throughout the United States. He received an M.S. in Art History from Pratt Institute, New York, and his M.F.A. in Painting at The University of Tulsa. For the past nine years, Nathan has been teaching studio art and art history courses for Oral Roberts University.

JAMES ANDREW SMITH attended the Kansas City Art Institute. He worked for ten years as a designer before formally beginning his art career in 2001. His work is exhibited in Tulsa through Joseph Gierek Gallery, and in galleries in Oklahoma City, Fort Worth, and Naples, Florida.

FRANCISCO TOLEDO, a Zapotec, was born in the Oaxaca region of Mexico. The etchings in this issue are from *Trece Maneras de Mirar um Mirlo,* a portfolio including ten drypoints published in 1981 by Galeria Arvil, Mexico City, and also appeared in *Nimrod*'s *Latin American Voices* issue of 1983. He has exhibited in galleries in Mexico, Europe, and South and North America. He was recently awarded the Right Livelihood Award for "devoting himself and his art to the protection and enhancement of the heritage, enviroment and community life of his native Oaxaca."

FUGUE

PAST CONTRIBUTORS

Steve Almond
Charles Baxter
Stephen Dobyns
Denise Duhamel
Stephen Dunn
Michael Martone
Campbell McGrath
W.S. Merwin
Sharon Olds
Jim Shepard
RT Smith
Virgil Suarez
Melanie Rae Thon
Natasha Trethewey
Anthony Varallo
Robert Wrigley
Dean Young

WIN

We award cash prizes and publication for prose and poetry in our annual spring contest. Past judges include Mark Doty, Rick Moody, Ellen Bryant Voight, Jo Ann Beard, Chris Abani, Rebecca McClanahan, and Tony Hoagland.

SUBMIT

Fugue invites submissions of fiction, creative nonfiction, poetry, drama, interview, and book reviews. Fugue is also home to The Experiment. Send SASE for guidelines or visit us on the web at http://www.uidaho.edu/fugue.

SUBSCRIBE

Individual
1 year/2 issues – $14
2 years/4 issues – $25
3 years/6 issues – $35
Institutional
1 year/2 issues – $22
2 years/4 issues – $40
3 years/6 issues – $55

FUGUE

PUBLISHED BY THE MFA PROGRAM AT THE UNIVERSITY OF IDAHO
200 BRINK HALL • UNIVERSITY OF IDAHO • P.O. BOX 441102, MOSCOW, IDAHO 83844

180